PHR Study

Guide

2023-2024

Review Book With 350 Practice
Questions and Answer Explanations
for the Professional in Human
Resources Certification

HANLEY
TEST PREPARATION

Contents

Free Video Offer!

Thank you for purchasing from Hanley Test Preparation! We're honored to help you prepare for your exam. To show our appreciation, we're offering an Exclusive Test Tips Video.

This video includes multiple strategies that will make you successful on your big exam.

All we ask is that you email us your feedback and describe your experience with our product. Amazing, awful, or just so-so. We want to hear what you have to say!

To get your FREE VIDEO, just send us an email at bonusvideo@hanleytestprep.com with **Free Video** in the subject line and the following information in the body of the email:

- The name of the product you purchased
- Your product rating on a scale of 1-5, with 5 being the highest rating.
- Your feedback about the product.

If you have any questions or concerns, please don't hesitate to contact us at support@hanleytestprep.com

Thanks again!

Introduction

'There are no secrets to success. It is the result of preparation, hard work, and learning from failure.'

– General Colin Powell (Wadsworth, 2021)

The Professional Human Resource (PHR) exam is a certification exam offered by the HR Certification Institute (HRCI) for individuals working in human resources (Passmall, 2022). The PHR exam assesses the knowledgeability of HR personnel in strategic management, risk management, workforce planning and employment, labor and employee relations, human resource development, and compensation and benefits (Passmall, 2022).

This certification is a great way for HR professionals to demonstrate their knowledge and expertise in the field and to advance their careers. The HRCI does not disclose exact figures on the number of people who take the PHR exam each year, but it is one of the organization's most popular certifications. This is understandable, especially when you consider the HRCI has issued over 500,000 professional certifications since it was founded.

The PHR exam is quite challenging, and it is not uncommon for people to take the exam more than once before they pass. The PHR exam has a pass rate of 65%, so more than half of those who take the exam fail on their first attempt (Passmall, 2022). A major reason for this is that the exam includes 175 questions chosen randomly from a pool of thousands of possible questions covering the entire HR field. The test is also scored on a curve, so the difficulty of the questions varies from one candidate to another.

As overwhelming as the process might seem, getting a certification like the PHR is a good way for any HR expert to stay competitive in their field and show their commitment to quality work (Smith, 2022). It will help you showcase your knowledge and skills to your employers, attract better compensation and potentially gain recognition within the HR community.

Maybe you lack the financial means to spend on review classes or professional tutors. Perhaps you have taken the PHR exam before without success. I am a human resources professional and I have spent years teaching aspiring professionals how to pass the PHR exam. Whatever your circumstances are, I believe that with hard work and discipline, you can pass this exam with flying colors. Focused study and preparation can not only help you pass the exam but also improve your job performance and expertise in your field.

Why this book?

I wrote this book to serve as a guide for anyone looking to sit for and pass the PHR exam. Not only do I want to share my knowledge and experience with you in this way, but I also wish to provide you with a review of the key concepts covered on the exam, including two full practice questions with answers. In a nutshell, here's what you'll learn in this book:

- Chapter One: Here you will learn all about the PHR exam, how it works, and the eligibility requirements. We will also discuss the content outline and some study habits you can adopt to help you prepare adequately for the exam.
- Chapter Two: You will learn all about the business management topics helpful in the HR profession. We will discuss the organizational structure of companies, regulatory processes, corporate governance, data reporting,

risk management, employee communications, and several other business elements of an organization.

- Chapter Three: Here, you will learn about the best hiring processes to find, attract, and employ top talent for your organization. We will discuss the relevant laws, staffing alternatives, interviewing techniques, workforce assessment, and the best ways to assess the effectiveness of a corporation's recruitment efforts.

- Chapter Four: We will discuss how you can apply and evaluate programs to help a company meet its goals. You will also learn about instructional design, organizational development methods, and how to encourage innovation within a company.

- Chapter Five: In this chapter, you will learn how to apply, promote, and manage reward schemes in strict adherence to all relevant regulations.

- Chapter Six: Here, we will discuss the largest section of the PHR exam. Specifically, you will learn how to implement initiatives and policies that would boost the experience of employees within your organization.

- Chapters Seven and Eight: These last two chapters would include two full-length practice tests with their detailed answers. The questions will test your understanding of everything we've discussed throughout this book and I hope you practice them as often as possible, alongside any other study materials you can access as you prepare for your exams.

Let's Get Started

It's never too early or too late to learn what you need to fully enrich your life. This book will help you ace the PHR exams and advance your career in human resources. It covers everything from recruitment and beneficial employee initiatives to risk management, applicable employment regulations, the role of an effective reward system, and how to guarantee the survival of your organization through succession planning. You will become more confident and familiar with the PHR examination questions each time you use it.

Excited? So am I. Take the first step by reading the rest of this book.

I'll be with you every step of the way.

Chapter One: The PHR Exam

Managing employees of any organization can help you create a good rapport with everyone, but this demands a certain set of abilities, particularly as managing people requires a degree of sophistication, empathy, and understanding. Fortunately, you can advance your HR career by sitting the PHR exam to get certified by HRCI.

Let's go through the PHR exam procedures and eligibility criteria in greater detail below.

Introduction to the PHR Exam

The HR Certification Institute created and maintains the Professional in Human Resources Exam to provide certifications to anyone looking to pursue a professional career in HR (HRCI, 2022). The HRCI is regarded as the leading provider of HR certifications on a global scale and before you register for the PHR, here are a few things you should consider:

When and Where is it Taken?

When your application to sit for this professional exam is accepted, the HRCI would issue you 'an eligibility ID'. Having this in your possession means that you have about 120 days (nearly four months) to prepare for and take your exam.

It is advised that you sign up for your exam as soon as possible to have some control over the time, date, and place of your choice. This is because there usually isn't enough room or seating to take all candidates and so, the spaces are filled in order of arrival.

In the case of an emergency, you can reschedule your exams for a fee. Otherwise, you will be deemed absent and forfeit all the money paid up to that time. If you cancel, you will receive a confirmation email with the date and time for the new scheduled exam.

What Should I Bring?

For this process, you would need your current, government-issued photo ID, your signature, a current photo that is easily recognizable, and your full name as it appears on your application (Passmall, 2022). Aside from these items, other personal properties such as mobile phones, food, beverages, watches, jewelry, or outerwear are prohibited from the test venue and may be placed in any available lockers or storage facilities during the exam.

What is Covered?

There are five primary components or functional areas covered by this computer-based test. You would also be expected to tackle 175 questions, but 25 of those questions will not count towards your final grade even though you must attempt all questions. Total exam time is usually three hours.

How is it Rated?

You'll receive a notification through your HRCI account once your result is uploaded and your scaled score will be published on your score report. This report will also contain details regarding how you performed on each of the exam's main sections. Use this as a reference for subsequent attempts if you were unsuccessful in the test.

f you don't pass the PHR the first time, try not to worry. You can schedule a retest after a 90-day waiting period, although you would need to reapply and pay another fee (Passmall, 2022). Only three exam retakes are permitted in a year, so be mindful of this. If you pass, you will receive information on how to get your digital badge, which serves as your official certification, along with your official exam results (Passmall, 2022). A paper certificate can also be made available to you for an extra charge, and this would bear the three-year expiration date of your PHR certification. To keep your certifications valid, you must complete at least 60 recertification credits within those three years or repeat the test (Passmall, 2022).

All that may sound overwhelming, but I've been there, and I know that with hard work and adequate preparations, you can ace this exam. Let us discuss the outline or the various components of the PHR exam, with their weighted scores, below.

Content Outline.

1. Business management (20%)

This component tests your ability to use your accumulated knowledge about a company and its business environment to influence the right decisions, reinforce expectations, and reduce risks (Passmall, 2022). According to the HRCI, to ace this part of the exam, you would need to show knowledge of:

- The organization's value system, mission, and structure.
- Legal and regulatory procedures and knowledge.
- Procedures for corporate governance and compliance.
- Communication among employees.
- Theory, techniques, and applications of change management.
- Efficient management of risks.
- Managing ambiguous, confusing, or chaotic circumstances.

2. Talent planning and acquisition (16%).

This aspect of the PHR is concerned with how well you can identify, attract, and recruit talent while adhering to all hiring-related federal requirements (Passmall,

2022). According to the HRCI, to ace this aspect of your test, you would need to demonstrate the following knowledge:

- Relevant federal rules and regulations that pertain to talent development and acquisition operations.
- Various personnel or staffing options (for example: knowing when to outsource, hire on a part-time basis or full-time).
- Processes for orienting or inducting new hires.
- Internal workforce evaluations. (for example, various forms of skills testing within the workforce).
- Transition strategies for business reorganization, M&A, thorough research, offshoring, as well as divestitures.
- Other useful metrics for evaluating past and prospective staffing effectiveness.

3. Development and Learning (10%).

Here, you would be tested on your ability to develop and assess programs, offer internal guidance, and relay data to help an organization's learning and growth efforts (Passmall, 2022). According to the HRCI, to pass this aspect of the test, you would need to show knowledge of:

- Learning and development theories and applications.
- All applicable federal rules and regulations relating to development schemes or activities.
- Facilitation, delivery, and tactics for training programs.
- Processes of adult learning.
- Methods and concepts for instructional design.
- and methods for measuring the success of training programs, using relevant metrics, amongst others.

4. Total rewards (15%).

This involves how well you can implement, promote, and monitor pay and benefits plans under all relevant federal rules or policies (Passmall, 2022). According to the HRCI, to pass, you need to know:

- Relevant federal rules and regulations about total rewards.
- Policies, procedures, and analysis relating to compensation.
- Payroll, accounting, and budgeting procedures about salary and benefits.
- Non-cash benefits.
- Techniques for coordinating and benchmarking pay and benefits.
- Policies, Procedures, and Analysis for Benefits Programs, etc

5. Labor and employee relations (39%)

This involves the management, observation, and/or advocacy for initiatives and policies that affect employee experience across the employee lifecycle that complies with the law (HRCI, 2022). According to the HRCI, to pass this section of the exam, you must show knowledge of:

- Basic employee relations activities and analysis (for example, undertaking investigations, investigating grievances, work environment reports, etc.)
- The relevant federal rules and regulations that impact employment, labor relations, safety, and security.
- Theories and applications of human interactions, cultures, and ideals to workers and organizations.
- Assessment and analysis procedure for rating employee satisfaction, attitudes, and opinions.
- Schemes or programs geared to encourage inclusivity and diversity within an organization.
- Data privacy and security.
- The performance management process, processes, and analysis.
- Collective bargaining.
- Termination strategies, ideas, terminologies, etc.

From personal experience, I know it can be quite challenging to study for an exam, particularly when you don't know where to start or what is expected of you. So what criteria must you meet as a candidate for the PHR certification? Let us discuss this further below:

Eligibility Requirements.

To qualify for the exam, the HRCI specifies you must hold a master's degree or higher, as well as a minimum of one year of professional experience in human resources (HRCI, 2022). You are also eligible if you have a bachelor's degree, with a minimum of two years of relevant work experience in the HR department.

If you cannot meet these conditions as well, you could still qualify to sit for the PHR exam if you have a minimum of 4 years experience in human resources and a high school diploma, or GED equivalent. These are non-transferable and non-refundable. After sending in your application successfully, all that would be left to do is prepare for the exam.

Study Habits To Success.

These study habits were pulled from Workforce Hub (2022) and Study Guide Zone (2022), and adopting them will help you prepare well for the PHR exam:

- **Self Assessment.**

  If you aren't as knowledgeable as needed in all weighted areas of the exam, how long will it take for you to be ready? You know your shortcomings and your learning speed better than anyone, so you must be honest with yourself here.

- **Make a study schedule**

  When you have a test date, depending on how prepared you are, create a study timeline to help you master all weighted areas of the test (Study Guide Zone, 2022). The biggest factor affecting your timing will be your schedule (Workforce Hub, 2022). So how much spare time do you have each week to study for exams? Schedule this into your weekly planner, boycott all forms of distractions, and practice.

- **Reassess your studying methods.**

Some people prefer to study for several minutes each day over a long time frame. Others prefer to study for longer hours or days at a stretch. What study techniques have yielded the most positive results for you in the past? If you have adopted no particular techniques before, which ones do you think would be suitable for you? Do you have an answer? Great! Now start studying.

- **Create a budget.**

You need to figure out your spending limit for items that you plan to buy besides your exam application and fee. This is very important because currently, the PHR exam fee is $395 and the application fee is $100. There are a few free resources available, but more comprehensive resources don't come cheap. While the HRCI does not advocate any particular programs for these studies, having a budget will help you manage and devote your resources to the areas you need help in. It would also help you avoid wastefulness.

- **Practice as much as possible.**

The HRCI, alongside many other study sites, provides a ton of PHR practice questions for candidates preparing for this test (Smith, 2022). Start practicing with these tests as early as possible. Your test results will show how well you studied. Review each question, including the ones you answered correctly and incorrectly. Study less in areas where you are strong and more in areas where you are weak (Smith, 2022).

- **Use technology to your advantage.**

You can prepare for the PHR with a variety of mobile applications and in-depth study materials (Sands, 2020). For instance: Evernote will make it easier for you to take notes, save images of study materials and clip web pages for easy access. Similarly, through the Pocket Prep app, you can access a thorough and adaptable study environment that focuses only on PHR test themes. The Quizlet program turns your notes into flashcards so you may use them to organize last-minute review sessions. This software also allows users to publish their flashcard sets, giving them access to study materials from previous successful PHR candidates (Sands, 2020).

- **Prepare "Outside the Box."**

The PHR requires traditional study, but it might not be enough because several of the questions could have more than one correct response and favor professional intuition over memory (Sands, 2020). For this reason, reach out to your colleagues who have taken this exam before. Sign up for PHR exam preparation classes or study groups. Immerse yourself in all things HR, working under the presumption that no such knowledge would be a waste.

On your exam day, get to the venue with hours to spare. The more time you have to relax at the venue, the more composed and calm you would be for your test.

During The Test.

- **Marking questions.**

Once the test begins, read through the questions as calmly as possible, going through each question twice or thrice. Look out for keywords; they are often very helpful because sometimes, more than one answer could be a good fit for a question. You don't have to answer all the questions at first glance, as you can mark the questions that you want to come back to. But if you do that, make sure you don't leave any questions unanswered.

- **The Clock.**

Although three hours may seem like a long time to finish the exam, time flies when you're under pressure. Remember that every time you glance at the time to confirm whether you are on track, you are taking your focus elsewhere. A compromise here is to check the clock after every ten questions. This way, you can maintain your attention on the topic at hand without getting sidetracked or losing track of time.

- **Answer questions strategically.**

Analyze the keywords in the questions to figure out the best-suited answer. When you don't know the answer to a question, there's no need to overthink it. You have a 25% chance of answering right, even with a blind guess. Start by eliminating the choices that you know are erroneous. Although it might not offer any new information, doing this will at the very least raise your chances (Sands, 2020).

- **Preparation Resources for PHR**

Finally, if you can afford to pay up to $700 for them, the HRCI study materials are a great choice for your preparation. You can create your customized package for a tailored curriculum using their many resources. Study.com, for instance, offers some 130 or more lessons, individual practice exams, and progress monitoring, and uses combined video courses and tests. It takes work to prepare for the PHR exam, but with careful planning, rigorous study, and a good test-day strategy, you can significantly increase your chances of passing and receiving your certification.

Key Takeaways:

- The HR Certification Institute (HRCI) created and maintains the Professional in Human Resources Exam to provide certifications to anyone looking to pursue a professional career in HR.
- There are five primary components or functional areas covered by this computer-based test. These include business management, learning and development, talent planning and acquisition, employee and labor relations, and total rewards.
- To qualify for the exam, you must hold a master's degree and a minimum of one year of professional experience in human resources, or a bachelor's degree and a minimum of 2 years of relevant work experience in the HR department, or a minimum of 4 years experience in human resources and a high school diploma, or GED equivalent.
- Practice as much as possible before your exam to build your confidence and expand your knowledge on all testing topics.

Now that you have this detailed overview of the PHR exam, what it entails, and the level of knowledge you must demonstrate for each functional area, we will discuss each one of these areas in more in-depth in the subsequent chapters of this book. In the next chapter, you will learn more about business management topics, useful in the HR profession.

Chapter Two: Business Management

As an HR professional, your business management skills are some of the best indicators of how useful you could be to any organization. When you understand the fundamentals of your organization's business operations, you are better equipped to strategically reshape the company's day-to-day activities and policies to serve its customers better. Let's get into more detail about the components of company management below:

Vision, Mission, Values, and the Structure of an Organization.

Both the mission and the vision of an organization relate to its purpose, and they are often expressed in writing. (Open Libraries, n.d). A mission statement explains the organization's purpose and how it intends to benefit its main stakeholders. The organization's mission and ambitions are more succinctly stated in the vision statement and are more focused on the future.

Values refer to ideals upheld by any organization. Together, the organization's mission and vision help build strategies, share that purpose with stakeholders, and shape the objectives and targets that will gauge whether the strategy is working.

The Organizational Structure.

A system that specifies how specific actions are to be carried out to accomplish an organization's objectives is known as an organizational structure (iEduNote, 2022). These are popularly used by successful companies across the globe because they clarify an organization's command chain. Each employee's role is described in a good organizational structure, along with how it fits into the larger system. A corporation can see how it is structured and how to best go forward in reaching its objectives thanks to this structuring.

- **Organizational Structures: Centralized versus Decentralized**

  The organizational structure of a company can either be centralized or decentralized. A decentralized structure distributes decision-making authority among several organizational levels, as opposed to a centralized system, which makes choices from the top down. The military is renowned for having a highly centralized organizational structure with a detailed and lengthy chain of leaders and subordinates. Aside from the aforementioned, there are a few other different organizational structures adopted by businesses across the globe (iEduNote, 2022). They comprise the following:

- **Functional Organizational Structure**

  This system divides a corporation according to the level of employee specialty and is also known as a bureaucratic structure. Most SME firms find it practical to adopt this structure. Here, the company is divided into departments that include branding, sales, marketing, and operations, amongst others.

- **(Multi) Divisional Organizational Structure**

  This is typical of large businesses with many business units. Here, the corporation is organized so that each business unit functions as a separate division with its own leader, despite having hundreds of products and business lines. Besides specialism, divisions can also be assigned a geographic location. For instance, a multinational firm might include divisions for North America and Asian divisions.

- **Team-Based Organizational Structure**

Identical to divisional or functional structures, team-based structured businesses divide their workforce into close-knit groups of staff to carry out specific tasks, but each group includes both leaders and workers.

- **Flat (Flatarchy) Organizational Structure**

A horizontal organization commonly referred to as flatarchy is more recent and is popular among entrepreneurs today. It evens out or flattens the hierarchical structure or chains of command in place and allows its staff a lot of independence, as the name suggests. Businesses that employ this structure have a rapid implementation rate.

- **Matrix Organizational Structure**

Companies may also be organized as a matrix. It is still the least used and most perplexing. Employees are cycled between many departments, divisions, and superiors under this system. For instance, a worker for a matrixed organization might be responsible for both customer service and sales.

- **Circular Organizational Structure**

Although they are hierarchical, these structures are so named because they set up senior staff members and managers in the center, with a concentric circle stretching outward to house lower-level staff members. The goal of this organizational structure is to promote teamwork and honest communication among the various tiers.

- **Network Organizational Structure**

Here, contractors and outside vendors are organized into networks to perform specific crucial tasks. Regardless of the structure adopted by your organization, the roles of every employee ought to be described in a good organizational structure, along with how it fits into the larger system. Companies can continue to operate effectively and strategically if HR recognizes the value of a solid organizational structure and implements one.

Legislative and Regulatory Knowledge and Procedures.

Laws start as ideas (bills) that must be sponsored (brought forward) by a representative (United States House of Representatives, n.d). A committee is then charged with studying the bill, after which it would be voted on, discussed, or altered before being approved. The approved bill goes to the Senate if it receives a simple majority approval vote (United States House of Representatives, n.d).

The bill is referred to another committee in the Senate and debated once again before being voted on. Once more, the bill is approved by a simple majority (here at least 51 of 100 members). Finally, any discrepancies between the House and Senate versions of the bill are resolved by a conference committee made up of members of both chambers. The resulting bill now goes back for final approval to the House and Senate. The updated measure is printed by the Government Printing Office through a procedure known as enrolling, and the President then has ten days to sign it or reject it.

According to the Legal Information Institute (n.d), administrative law is the body of laws and legal doctrines guiding how government agencies are run and regulated. The enactment of federal laws necessitates the establishment of agencies whose roles are to interpret, implement, and execute those laws under the agency's organic statutes (Legal Information Institute, n.d).

- **Lobbying.**

  Trying to promote, oppose, or in any other way shape or trying to influence the introduction, rejection, or enactment of laws before any legislative body is known as lobbying (National Conference of State Legislatures 2022). States often describe lobbying as an effort to sway policy through written or verbal communication. Each nation may have its own definitions of lobbying, as well as exceptions to those definitions.

- **Corporate Governance Compliance and Procedures.**

  Organizations typically set up rules, regulations, and processes called "corporate governance practices" to guide their operations and control risk (TPI

Group Inc., 2019). These must comply with the moral requirements and fiduciary obligations of the company's compliance environment, which are ensured by good corporate governance policies.

- **Practice versus Principle.**

Corporate compliance is the collection of practical acts necessary to engage in the business world if corporate governance is the philosophy that directs conduct. This entails making sure that corporate procedures comply with legal requirements, which frequently require consulting outside experts. For instance, rather than burdening internal departments, technical issues like financial reporting, tax filing, and tax record management should be farmed out to a tax specialist (TPI Group Inc. 2019).

- **Differences Between Governance and Compliance**

Corporate governance adopts a long-term perspective and is concentrated on enhancing future business performance (TPI Group Inc. 2019). Since businesses may need to abide by a wide range of rules and regulations to deliver their goods and services, compliance issues are considerably more practical.

Another way to view these two aspects of business is that on the one hand, corporate board members develop governance policies to safeguard the future and current interests of shareholders. Compliance policies are necessary for organizations to function legally and in compliance with federal regulations to avoid legal penalties.

Corporate Governance Structure & Principles (TPI Group Inc. 2019).

Whatever the circumstance, businesses need to be equipped to deal with a wide range of problems. As a smart HR professional, this is where you come in. Some of the best policies for good corporate governance that you can help your organization adopt or improve on include:

- Systems for monitoring and reporting business performance.

- An explicitly defined working relationship and responsibility allocation between top executives and the company's president or CEO.
- Regulations governing the appointment of the company's directors.
- Rules governing the ethics of corporate behavior.
- Principles for financial reporting and both internal and external communications.

Considerations for Corporate Compliance (TPI Group Inc. 2019).

Companies must preserve enough documents to show that they are undertaking business under all the rules and regulations in the current financial environment. In actuality, this paperwork may comprise:

- Constitutional documents (such as the Articles and Memorandum of Association).
- Records of the annual meetings of directors and shareholders.
- Ownership, dividend, and transaction details for the stock.
- Documented resolutions relating to corporate governance.
- List of business transactions and service suppliers.
- Documents pertaining to taxes, and any other additional documents or records of business that could be demanded by the laws operational within your community or industry.

Employee Communications.

This entails the exchange of thoughts, feelings, and information between staff members and management inside an organization (First Up Blog, n.d.). It can take place verbally or virtually via a variety of platforms, including intranets, smartphone applications, and collaborative tools. Setting clear objectives that can spark a passion for your company's mission and vision in your staff is necessary for effective communication.

Professional and Ethical Standards.

The ethical standards that direct choices and behavior at a business or organization are outlined in the code of ethics and professional conduct (Betterteam, 2022). They provide both broad guidelines for acceptable behavior by employees and detailed instructions for dealing with problems like harassment, safety, and conflict of interest.

According to Leonard (2018), every organization should have its baseline standard of ethics and expectations. These might deal with the acceptable dress code, punctuality, workplace harassment, the application process for leaves of absence, etc. Those who violate a company's ethics policies typically face disciplinary action, including termination (Leonard, 2018).

Setting clear ethical and professional standards at work is crucial for a variety of reasons. When dealing with a company, people and consumers feel secure because they know everyone is abiding by morally upright standards. It enhances the company's reputation and conducts "clean business" or prioritizes "customers." Ethics standards also establish the tone for how businesses handle internal disagreements. This significantly contributes to the productivity and happiness of the staff.

Business Elements of an Organization

The organizational structure establishes a strategy for future efficient growth while also displaying corporate communication and the executive and management hierarchy. The following are the six fundamental components of organizational structure (iEduNote, 2022):

- Designing jobs: This means defining a person's work obligations, outlining areas of decision-making accountability, setting expectations and goals, and choosing the right performance metrics.
- Grouping or departmentalizing jobs: This refers to the effective coordination of multiple tasks to meet the goals of the organization as quickly as possible.
- Creation of effective reporting relationships between jobs: This shows a clear, identifiable hierarchy of authority amongst positions and specifies

the proportion of employees who are accountable to a specific leader. It also clarifies the management hierarchy and management.

- Assignment of authority among job positions: A supply manager may have the authority to monitor the delivery of goods to a company's warehouse, assess and record the quality of the goods supplied, and provide reports to the CFO on his findings. However, he should not decide on the sales price for them.
- Coordination of tasks between jobs: If each person is allowed to carry out their task effectively without considering the related task being carried out by another person, chaos would reign in the organization.
- Differentiating between many positions: A company's organizational structure must reflect the distinction between line and staff positions. The degree to which these positions are distinct and well-defined will determine how productive the company is as a whole.

Reporting and Analysis of Data

Data reporting and analysis are essential elements of corporate management and play a big role in a company's success (Express Analytics, 2021). Reporting entails processing and sharing information about a company or its surroundings. The process of data analysis is more focused on the actual corporate goals than data reporting typically is (Jedox blog, n.d). It explains the procedure of analyzing data and reporting to provide insightful findings that can help comprehend and enhance business performance.

Why Is Data Analysis and Reporting Important?

Reporting frequently entails tedious data entry procedures involving large volumes of information. Analysis demands a more individualized strategy that blends analytical techniques with the abilities of someone like a data analyst (Express Analytics, 2021). It involves gaining knowledge to present effective steps to accomplish a particular goal.

Therefore, whereas reporting can connect many data sources, permit comparisons, and make information easier to understand, the analysis evaluates that information and suggests a course of action. This is a major factor in the rising demand for data analysts, as businesses of all sizes should be able to advise management on how to go forward with their operations.

Being a good human resource manager entails taking all the steps to help your organization adapt to changes. Your company needs a good change management framework if it aims to plan its change initiatives early enough to help its personnel adjust to the same. Let's discuss this further below:

Change Management Structure.

The theory of change management provides a framework for reshaping people, procedures, and resources to get better results (Altadonna, 2022). The central idea here is to help organizations concentrate on what's ahead and make the best decisions to realize their vision. Some of the best change management theories include:

1. The change management philosophy of Kotter.

Kotter (1996) proposes an 8-step procedure for organizational change in his book "Leading Change":

- Establishment of a sense of urgency.
- Creation of a governing coalition.
- Establishment of a strategic vision.
- Description of the vision.
- Elimination of obstacles to encourage activity.
- Creation of quick victories.
- Maintenance of acceleration.
- Anchoring shifts in the workplace.

Given how well it creates a feeling of urgency and explains why change is necessary, Kotter's organizational change theory is one of the most well-known change management approaches.. Kotter adopts a top-down strategy. If you begin with these stages, include some strategies for generating support from the public and getting input from front-line staff.

2. The 7-S change management model from McKinsey (2008).

The model emphasizes coordination over structure and lays out several interrelated aspects that affect a company's capacity for change. These seven components include hard elements, such as:

- Your strategy: This is your game plan for competing and winning in the market.
- Structure: This is your organizational framework, including your reporting structure.
- Systems: These are the procedures and tools that personnel use to complete their tasks.

It also includes soft elements.

- Shared values: fundamental principles that the organization's work ethic and corporate culture define.
- Style: refers to a leadership style used to manage the business and its staff.
- Staff: The people who work for the company.
- Skills: Which refers to the collective skills and expertise set of employees.

The 7-S model excels at helping businesses understand the workings of their current operating system so they can easily spot the areas that must be changed. The model also aids by illustrating the extent to which a company's structural changes may affect every one of the seven components.

3. The Nudge Management Model

Richard H. Thaler and Cass R. Sunstein (2008) outlined the ideas for this theory in their book *Nudge: Improving Decisions About Health, Wealth, and Happiness.* Just like the word 'nudge' implies, this change management theory posits the gentle encouragement of people to change without enforcing severe rules or punishing non-compliance. To increase the likelihood that your staff will comply with the new rules in place, it is more helpful sometimes to offer the change as an adjustment option to employees, not a mandate. This will make it easier for your organization to highlight the advantages of the transition and celebrate minor victories. Companies going through major organizational changes may find this approach helpful.

4. The Kübler-Ross Change Curve

This change management model is based on the work of psychiatrist Elisabeth Kübler-Ross (1969) on the five stages of mourning. She described that people who are terminally ill typically process their feelings about their impending deaths in five stages -denial, anger, bargaining, depression, and acceptance. So why is grief theory included in a list of business change management models? Well, people are by nature averse to change. The five stages of mourning are expanded upon by the change curve to represent the feelings employees experience as they adjust to an organizational change. This can be a fantastic tool for considering and controlling how your employees will respond to a change..

Risk Management

This encompasses the identification, evaluation, and control of risks to ensure the stability and continued progress of a company (Western Governor's University, 2020). As a leader in your organization, you would have to consider all trouble spots, consider the best remedies for a difficult situation, and then put procedures in place to help to the greatest extent decrease those risks. Fortunately, there are many risk management strategies your business may use to reduce risk. Some of these methods comprise:

- **Risk avoidance:** With this method, you just avoid the risk entirely. For instance, businesses that want to minimize the risk of unprofessional conduct amongst staff often conduct background checks on new hires. The same thing happens when an investor decides against investing in a sector of the economy that is losing money.
- **The transfer of risk;** A corporation transfers risk when it recognizes that it faces a risk that it cannot eliminate and seeks the help of an insurance provider or other third party to help it manage that risk. For instance, when a business enters into contracts with clients or employees through a legal corporation, it is transferring risk and helps to mitigate any potential future risk.

- **Loss prevention:** When a business realizes there are some risks it cannot eliminate, it can minimize loss by putting preventative measures in place to lessen the impact of those risks. For instance, a business might mandate passwords for computer users to protect sensitive data and company information.
- **Risk-retention:** This method entails managing risk within your organization as opposed to depending on outside sources. An organization that manages its computer security internally, as opposed to using a 3rd party company or software, is an example of retaining risk.
- **Distributing or spreading the risk:** To spread out the risk of their huge clients, insurance companies often choose to partner with other successful companies. This is a great example of risk distribution because when the chips are down, the corporation would then distribute the insurance with those other companies.

Although risks are unavoidable aspects of doing business, it's crucial to devise a strategy for your risk response to keep your firm secure. To be successful, business owners and leaders must comprehend risk management and have a strategy in place.

Qualitative and Quantitative Methods and Tools for Analytics.

These are the two main categories of information you might gather for market research, and both can be useful for various objectives (Michigan University Online, 2019). In quantitative research, numbers are everything and they portray crucial information about your company. Qualitative research focuses more on people and their perceptions of your company than it does on numbers. This is frequently done by interviewing individuals or groups of people and helps business define their challenges by gaining insight into the attitudes, values, and beliefs of their target market.

Qualitative research asks lengthy questions that start with "how" and "why," while quantitative research involves pointed questions that start with "to what extent," "how much," and "how many." Examples of questions arising from qualitative research are: Why do you feel this product outperforms its rivals? Why do you believe it doesn't? How do you feel about this new business logo? How do you feel about this print advertisement?

Dealing With Chaotic, Unclear, or Confusing Situations.

All organizations have to deal with uncertainty from time to time. Your best foot forward as a professional HR personnel is to help your organization embrace those confusing situations, understand how they arose, and handle them decisively (Forbes Coaches Council, 2020). Here are some helpful tips:

- **Incorporate flexibility.**

  The more flexible you are in the wake of chaos, the quicker you can decide your organization needs to survive.

- **Be open and honest.**

  Watch out for lessons that can help you find some order in the chaos or some insight into confusion. Being honest and remaining teachable through it all is what sets an outstanding leader apart from the rest.

- **Implement and improve**

  Some solutions will fail, and that's okay. Don't berate yourself for coming up with imperfect ideas. Choose instead to work on and improve on them, reaching out to experts in your field to help you along the way.

- **Exercise open communication**

  Finally, understand that people need reliable and reputable sources of information during unsettled times and your staff is no exemption. Transparent leaders foster trust and boost worker confidence during tumultuous times, and you should always encourage your management to take this stance when the going gets tough.

Key Takeaways:

- As an HR professional, your business management skills are some of the best indicators of how useful you could be to any organization.
- A system that specifies how specific actions are to be carried out to accomplish an organization's objectives is known as an organizational structure.
- The theory of change management provides a framework for reshaping people, procedures, and resources to get better results.
- As a leader in your organization, you would have to consider all trouble spots, consider the best remedies for a difficult situation, and then put procedures in place to help to the greatest extent decrease those risks.
- As a professional HR personnel, you are tasked with helping your organization embrace confusing situations, understand how they arose, and tackle all attendant issues from same decisively.

As a leader, I can tell you from personal experience that employing and keeping the right talent for your organization is easier said than done. Still, you can make the process all work out for your company. To do this, though, you must factor in certain considerations throughout the recruitment process. Let us discuss this further in the next chapter.

Chapter Three: Talent Planning and Acquisition

Employees favor organizations with positive cultures, competitive salaries, and possibilities for progression in a healthy employment market (Open Libraries, n.d). It takes time and a systematic approach to personnel planning and acquisition for an organization to gain a reputation as one that workers desire to work for. Let's discuss this aspect of your duties as an HR professional below:

Applicable Federal Laws and Regulations to Talent Planning and Acquisition.

Understanding and applying the law in all actions the HR department conducts is one of the most crucial aspects of HRM (University of Illinois Board of Trustees, 2022). The law is extremely clear about employment practices, specifically on fair hiring that includes all people who apply for jobs.

Certain laws are outlined by the University of Illinois Board of Trustees (2022) to cover hiring new employees and they include:

- **Immigration Reform and Control Act (United States Congress, 1986)**

  Employers are required by law to verify the immigration status of their staff members. It is unlawful to recruit or hire illegal immigrants. This is why the question "Do you have the right to work within the United States?" appears on many job applications.

The IRCA applies to both subcontractors and the employees you hire. If it is proven that your company exerts control over how and when the subcontractors fulfill their duties, you could still be held accountable in a subcontractor scenario (for example, if your company hires an outside company to clean the facility after hours).

Even temporary employees are subject to identity and job eligibility verification by HR personnel. The reporting form used to determine a worker's identity and lawful employment status is the INS I-9 form (Employment Eligibility Verification form). The second component of the I-9 form must be completed within three days of the first day of employment, and employers must have the employee complete it on their first day of work.

- **The Patriot Act (United States Congress, 2001)**

The Patriot Act was passed because of the terrorist events on September 11, 2001, and increased the federal government's capacity to carry out surveillance operations. For instance, the government can access voicemail and email correspondence with just a search warrant. If staff is suspected of supporting terrorism, the government may inspect communications and is not required to inform the employer that it is doing so. Before the employment process gets started, HR experts and managers should inform candidates of these new standards.

- **The Equal Pay Act (United States Congress, 1963)**

This law prohibits gender-based discrimination in the payment of wages or benefits when men and women work for the same employer under comparable working conditions and are required to use similar skills, effort, and responsibility.

The EEOC is the agency tasked with executing federal employment discrimination statutes in the workplace (U.S. Equal Employment Opportunity Commission, n.d) . While there are limitations to the kinds of businesses that are protected (those with at least 15 employees), the EEOC is still required to collect data and look into discrimination complaints for businesses with over 15 staff. Employers are prohibited from discriminating in the hiring process under EEO laws based on age (40 years of age or older), handicap, genetic information, nationality, sex, pregnancy, race, and religion.

Organizations typically include an EEO statement in job postings. HR is expected to display notices of EEOC regulations in a conspicuous area of the workplace, besides including the EEO policy in the job announcement (such as the break room).

Although the EEOC's employment regulations prohibit discrimination, a situation known as a bona legitimate occupational requirement may arise (BFOQ). A BFOQ is a characteristic or attribute that can be used to evaluate applicants and is deemed to be fairly required for the regular operation of the business. BFOQ exceptions can take the following forms:

- A teacher in a private religious school might need to belong to the same religion as the students or employer.
- When they reach a particular age, airline pilots must take mandatory retirement.
- Only male models may be employed by a clothing retailer that sells men's apparel.
- It may not be necessary for a restaurant to recruit male servers if the theme of the establishment depends on one sex over another (like Hooters).

- **Age Discrimination in Employment Act (United States Congress, 1967)**

This law forbids discrimination against those who are 40 years of age or older, encourages the hiring, advancement, and other terms and conditions of employment of older people, and mandates that hiring choices be made based on qualifications rather than age.

- **Americans with Disabilities Act (United States Congress, 1990)**

This law forbids the exclusion of qualified applicants who can perform the "essential functions" of the job without help or with "reasonable accommodation," mandates that facilities be accessible to the disabled, outlaws employment discrimination based on disability, and forbids pre-employment medical inquiries and examinations.

- **Federal Executive Order #11246 (Executive Order, 1965)**

This statute mandates positive affirmative action from government contractors to remedy a lack of representation or exclusion in the workforce on grounds of race, gender, or ethnicity.

- **Illinois Human Rights Act (Illinois General Assembly, 2021)**

This act guarantees the right to work without being subjected to discrimination based on race, color, religion, sex, national origin, ancestry, age, marital status, physical or mental disability, military status, or an undesirable military discharge.

- **Pregnancy Discrimination Act (United States Congress, 1978)**

Pregnancy-based discrimination is forbidden under this. It states that for other employment-related considerations, such as fringe benefits, pregnant employees will receive the same treatment as non-pregnant employees.

- **Title VII of the Civil Rights Act (United States Congress, 1964)**

This law prohibits discrimination based on race, religion, color, sex, or national origin in hiring, salary, and other terms, conditions, or privileges of employment.

Planning Concepts and Terms: Succession Planning (Kenton, 2022).

Succession planning is a popular strategy to ensure the smooth transfer of leadership responsibilities from one member of staff to another (Kenton, 2022). When used well, not only does succession planning guarantee the survival of a company, but it also empowers employees by equipping them with the skill set they need to grow in the industry.

Succession planning is often long-term oriented. The entire process can take anywhere from 12 to 36 months to complete because it typically encompasses the proper recruitment of top talents and extensive training. Staff members must be thoroughly trained not just to suit their current responsibilities, but also to function across all other departments within the company. This would help employees improve their employability skills, to advance their careers.

There are several advantages to succession planning and these include the following:

- When workers are conscious of their opportunities for advancement, their sense of empowerment and job satisfaction might rise.
- The provision of plans for future promotions supports employee career advancement and makes employees feel appreciated.
- Through succession planning, organizations can coach members of staff to pass on skills and expertise from one leadership team to the next.
- Through the process, the management could obtain and preserve employee records and track the contribution of their staff so that job openings can be filled by existing staff as they arise.
- The more staff members interact with the management through succession planning, the greater their chances of identifying with and sharing the company's values and mission.

Workplace Planning

To prevent prospective shortages or surpluses of human capital, workforce planning is a methodical process that proactively analyzes current workforce gaps and projects' future staffing needs. The idea here is that a business can staff more effectively if it takes the initiative to routinely assess and project both its future needs. Benefits of workforce planning include:

- Rapid replacement of talent: Being able to quickly fill jobs left empty by unexpected (or unavoidable) personnel turnover so that services or products don't suffer (Farrugia, 2022).
- An orderly business cycle: By creating procedures that function well in both prosperous and difficult economic periods, you can even out the cycles.

- Lower turnover rates: Workers are continually prepared for new chances that match their interests and skills in terms of their careers. They adapt to them quickly and effortlessly.
- Lower labor costs: This is because workplace planning guarantees that the right personnel are employed, at the right time, in the right location, and are managed effectively, all with no significant layoffs.
- Future layoffs will be less frequent because headcount management prevents a talent surplus in the organization. There are also more internal opportunities.

Workforce planning is effective because it makes everyone think forward and eliminates surprises. A workforce planning model often includes the following components:

- Workforce Analysis: A study of the organization's labor force and demands, as well as a projection of upcoming workforce requirements and needs.
- Staffing Gap Analysis: The process of identifying gaps in the current workforce supply and demand, as well as the company's current capacity to foresee future changes in workforce requirements.
- Solution Deployment: Putting a plan to fill personnel gaps into action.
- Performance evaluation: Keeping track of key performance indicators to make sure the workforce plan satisfies corporate requirements.

Current Market Situation and Talent Pool Availability

Think of a talent pool as a record of prospective employees maintained to help an organization nurture and keep its connections with individuals whose talents and knowledge match those of the company's competencies and values (Smart Recruiters, n.d.). Maintaining a talent pool is vital because, with such a collection of highly skilled people who are already acquainted with and interested in your firm, your company can easily draw from the pool anytime a vacancy opens up in your business, without having to invite new applications.

Staffing Alternatives

Conventional hiring practices like in-person interviews, paper applications, and full-time job offers with specified hours (usually 9 am-5 pm) are referred to as traditional staffing methods. To set yourself apart from your peers as an HR professional, you need to keep up with the times and figure out the best staffing alternatives to traditional staffing that your company can adopt to attract the best talents in your industry (Kempton, 2022). Examples of these alternatives are: recruiting through a verified staffing agency, outsourcing particular projects, providing possibilities for internships, and employing freelancers as part of your team (Kempton, 2022).

Interviewing and Selection Techniques

There are several techniques for interviewing and selecting the finest applicants for roles within your organization (Challenge Consulting, n.d). The most popular ones include the following:

- **Preliminary Screening:** Here, the recruiter decides which candidates to call for the initial screening after having reviewed the applications sent in for the positions.
- **Telephone Interview:** The applicants who could express their abilities and qualifications in a way that satisfies the company's employment needs are normally chosen by the recruiter after this interview for a face-to-face meeting.
- **Interviews in person:** By this stage, the application pool is often already reduced to a handful of finalists reduced after the preliminary screening and phone interviews.
- **Selection based on cultural fit:** Here, the handful of finalists is reduced further to include only the candidates whose values are like that of the hiring company.
- **Candidate vetting:** Here, the recruiter sends the top applicant a conditional job offer, performs background checks, and administers drug tests. A final offer is sent out to the candidate who clears the background investigation and drug test.

Applicant Tracking Systems

The ATS is software designed to spot specific keywords in resumes to eliminate applications that don't match the job description (Henderson, 2022). You can integrate this system into your recruitment process easily because it saves time and makes the job of short-listing the best candidates relatively easier than before. The main issue with the ATS, though, is that more qualified candidates may be eliminated if their resumes lack the keywords inputted into the tracking system.

The Impact of Total Rewards on Recruitment and Retention

A total rewards strategy refers to any effort made by an organization to create an engaged workforce that grows alongside the company through an efficient and all-encompassing incentives program (Gardner, 2022). A total rewards strategy is composed of five components, including:

- **Compensation:** This covers the benefits that empower workers, including base salary, variable pay, stock options, and cash bonuses.
- **Benefits:** These are the packages offered to employees to improve their level of personal, societal, and family security. Examples are retirement programs, leave policies, life, health, and disability insurance, etc
- **Wellbeing:** Organizational cultures that encourage and foster employee well-being can be identified by things like employee assistance programs, flexible work schedules, etc.
- **Recognition:** Your company staff would feel appreciated the more their accomplishments are acknowledged. This can happen through awards, promotions, verbal thanks, or even simple acts of respect.
- **Employee development programs:** These are investments made by employers to assist their staff to rise within the company and reach their full potential.

A total rewards system encourages performance excellence, increasing an organization's ability to compete in the market. It also ensures that your company keeps achieving its goals by finding and keeping its talented personnel.

Processes and Procedures for Candidate Testing

Employers can screen and assess prospective employees using a variety of efficient tools and methods. The following is a sum of the major phases through which you can choose the best candidates for an open position within your company:

- Start by figuring out the basic requirements of the role.
- Pre-screen to weed out applicants with unsuitable qualifications for the job.
- Conduct a preliminary evaluation to further weed out applicants without the required level of abilities and competencies.
- The selection of candidates with the best chance of succeeding on the job should take place after you've conducted a thorough evaluation through interviews and job simulations.
- Finally, verify the job history and credentials of your finalists and send out your offer to the best candidates. (SHRM, 2022)

Techniques for Verbal and Written Contracts

An agreement between an employer and an employer governing the length of the employment is known as an employment contract (Guerin, 2022). This could be implied by law, written (formal), or verbal.

- **Implied Contracts:** An implied contract is an agreement that was not reduced in writing, or even verbalized. Rather, the existence of the agreement is inferred from the conduct of the employer, both spoken and unspoken.
- **Oral Contracts:** A verbal agreement that is not recorded in writing is referred to as an oral contract. They can be difficult to prove in the law courts, but oral agreements are just as legally binding as written ones.
- **Written Contracts:** These are official or formal agreements, which clearly outline the conditions of employment, the benefits and duties of both parties to the contract, and the conditions under which the employment agreement can be terminated. Once signed and sealed, such formal contracts become legally binding on both employer and employee.

Once there is a valid employment agreement between your organization and a new recruit, you'd best turn your attention to conducting orientation for the new staff.

Employment Orientation for New Hires (Verlinden, 2022)

This refers to the process of acclimating new hires to their positions, coworkers, and the company (Verlinden, 2022). Giving new hires a tour of the office space, introducing them to the team, setting up their email accounts, sharing the Wi-Fi password, and other such practicalities are all part of the process.

A well-organized orientation program makes new employees feel less anxious and stressed and at ease with their new roles. Along with boosting productivity and loyalty to the company, it should also help to lower turnover and the rate at which mistakes are made as the employees discharge their responsibilities.

Internal Workforce Assessment (Bamboo HR, 2022).

Workforce analysis is the process of analyzing staff data to make better decisions about the hiring, retention, and management of employees. The goal of a workforce assessment is to maintain the right staffing levels for the achievement of key competencies, effective succession management, cost optimization, and resilience. As an HR professional, it is your responsibility to balance creating an engaging experience for your applicants and hiring the best person for the job. And that is where skill testing comes in.

What is a Skill Test?

A skill test is an assessment that gives a candidate's ability to carry out the tasks mentioned in the job description, an objective, extensive evaluation (Garland, 2022). A good skills exam should also have questions that can be answered by someone who is already performing the job to enable you to measure all the important performance indicators for the role in question as accurately as possible.

We have highlighted several components of your talent planning and acquisition role, but only as it relates to the recruitment of employees. Another vital aspect of your role is handling employee transitions as they occur. Let us briefly discuss the best techniques for this below:

Transition Techniques.

People go through several stages as they transition from one role to the next: letting go of the former behaviors, a period of uncertainty, and a fresh start with new behaviors. It's important to communicate and rely on clear transition plans, especially in those situations where an employee suddenly resigns.

What is an Employee Transition Plan?

Think of this as a document detailing the changes that can occur in a company's organizational structure because of an employee's resignation or transition from one role to another (University of Michigan Medical School, 2022). A transition plan helps in streamlining all processes and in finding some order in an otherwise chaotic event. Follow these seven tips to create a good staff transition plan for transitioning staff members within your organization:

- Create an organizer to compile all the information on a transitioning employee into a single, useful document.
- Request support from the transferring employee where necessary so that they have the chance to help ease the burden of the transition.
- Choose who needs to be informed about the change and update everyone else on a need-to-know basis.
- Choose a replacement for the vacant role to speed up the process.
- Schedule some time to collect feedback. An exit interview, for instance, can show you where your company needs to improve, and how you can plan better for future transitions.
- Come up with an employees' communication strategy to maintain information flow and keep everyone at ease.
- Help the transitioning employee make or maintain a good impression. You can, for instance, create an avenue for their teammates to express

their gratitude to the departing employee, or organize a send-forth party for them.

Metrics to Evaluate Past and Future Staffing Effectiveness (Vulpen, 2022)

You can adopt certain metrics throughout your talent acquisition process to help your organization track a candidate's success and streamline its hiring processes (Vulpen, 2022). The most important of such metrics include:

- **Time to fill:** This measures the period between the time a job application is approved and when the candidate accepts your offer to fill in the advertised vacant post.
- **Time to hire:** The time it takes for a candidate to get hired after they have applied is known as the "time to hire."
- **Source of hire:** One of the most common recruiting metrics is keeping track of the sources that bring in new hires to your company. This measure aids in monitoring the efficiency of various recruiting channels.
- **First-year attrition:** First-year attrition can either be managed or unmanaged. Managed attrition refers to the employing organization terminating the employment agreement. Unmanaged attrition describes a situation where an employee quits on their own. The former is frequently a sign of poor first-year performance or poor team fit.
- **Hire quality:** A candidate's first-year success can be predicted by the hiring quality, which is frequently determined by a person's performance rating. Candidates with high-performance ratings are a sign of successful hiring, while candidates with low-performance ratings are the opposite (Vulpen, 2022).

Key Takeaways:

- Understanding and applying the law in all actions the HR department conducts is one of the most crucial aspects of HRM.
- Succession planning is a process that ensures the smooth transfer of leadership responsibilities from one member of staff to another in the interim, as well as in the future.
- To set yourself apart from your peers as an HR professional, you need to keep up with the times and figure out the best staffing alternatives to traditional staffing that your company can adopt to attract the best talents in your industry.
- You can adopt certain metrics throughout your talent acquisition process to help your organization track a candidate's success and streamline its hiring processes.

Now that you know about how to acquire the best talents for your organization, in the next chapter, you will learn all about applying, evaluating programs, and providing consultation and data to contribute to your organization's learning and development actions.

Chapter Four: Learning and Developments

There is no one-size-fits-all for HR responsibilities. As a professional, you would have to make decisions that may attract serious legal repercussions for your organization. That is why you need to understand the development programs your company needs to grow while also operating within the confines of the law (Joubert, 2020). Let us discuss this further below:

Federal Laws for Learning and Development (Joubert, 2020).

- **Laws against workplace discrimination**

  There are various laws that forbid discrimination on grounds of age, handicap, genetic data, nationality, race or ethnicity, gender, pregnancy, or religious beliefs. The Pregnancy Discrimination Act (United States Congress, 1978), the Equal Pay Act (United States Congress, 1963), the Americans with Disabilities Act (United States Congress, 1990), and the Age Discrimination in Employment Act (United States Congress, 1967), are all relevant here and you must always adhere to their provisions.

- **Laws governing wages**

The current Fair Labor Standards Act (United States Congress, 1938) is a vital enactment, as it stipulates what the federal minimum wage is. The Family and Medical Leave Act (United States Congress, 1993) provides for unpaid leave with job protection and continued access to healthcare. Providing veterans and active soldiers with more legal protections also includes expanded flexibility for them.

- **Laws governing employee benefits**

There are laws enacted to defend the rights of workers to various benefits. For instance, The Employee Retirement Income Security Act (United States Congress, 1974) stipulates the conditions a company must fulfill before it can provide its staff with pension plans. Other laws relevant here are the Health Insurance Portability and Accountability Act (United States Congress, 1996), the Patent Protection and Affordable Care Act, also known as "Obamacare" (United States Congress, 2010), and the Consolidated Omnibus Budget Reconciliation Act (United States Congress, 1985).

- **Immigration laws**

Employers are required to hire only individuals who are authorized to work in the United States by immigration laws, such as the Immigration and Nationality Act (United States Congress, 1965). It's also crucial that businesses observe anti-discrimination regulations as they check applicants' eligibility for employment.

- **Laws governing workplace safety**

The Occupational Safety and Health Administration (OSHA, 1970) is in place to guarantee workers' access to safe working environments. It describes and regulates the administration of programs that assist government employees who sustained injury while performing their work tasks.

You must show the ability to understand, evaluate and implement the law at all times in your duty as an HR professional. Not only would this help you stand out from the crowd and benefit your organization, but it would also help you advance your career

Learning and Development Theories and Applications.

Now, besides your compliance with the law, your success as a leader also depends on how well you encourage constant improvement in every staff member within your organization. According to EduFixers (n.d), in the HRM field, the process of strategic training is governed by four primary learning theories. These include:

- **Behaviorist Theory**

  According to this theory, the best types of training combine the positive alongside the negative effects that can eventually lead to a change in behavior. Behaviorism may be applied in task-oriented HRM settings by rewarding a trainee who successfully gained a new skill or criticizing those who fail.

- **Cognitive Theory**

  Within the context of this theory, existing knowledge stimulates the cognitive process, allowing it to expand learning by strengthening the knowledge base. Training based on this approach would improve employees' capacity for critical and logical thought and their ability to solve difficulties practically.

- **Constructivist Theory**

  According to this approach, an HR training program would incorporate learning strategies such as participation in forum discussions, feedback forms, and various other forms of contribution by the employees being trained. The assumption here is that employees are capable of self-directed learning and continuous performance development.

- **Connectivism Theory**

  This theory is based on the idea that, to make information credible, connections must be made between various sources of information. Connectivism also describes the relationships between various individuals involved in comparable activities to foster a fruitful exchange of experiences (EduFixers, n.d).

Training Program Facilitation, Techniques, and Delivery

Creating a training program requires considering many important factors (Open Libraries, n.d). This is because employee training should be tailored to foster the growth of the employees and the organization. Will it take a day or an hour to deliver the training? How will you invite employees to the training? Would you publish the details of the program on your slack channel, or send off personalized emails?

The proposed delivery method and the lecture content in such training programs also matter. Before creating the content, be sure to establish the training's learning objectives and goals to create a better experience for the trainees.

The last step in creating a training framework is to think about how it will be evaluated. How will you determine if the trainees actually learned something in the end? Working out these details ahead of time can help you provide immense value to your staff, which can help you keep the best employees for the organization.

Adult Learning Processes

There are different learning processes through which professional growth can be achieved in the workplace (Mometrix Test Preparation, 2022). Some of these include:

- **Administration of literary education through lectures:** Industry experts are often invited to companies to affect knowledge through this process. This type of training may instruct in basic reading and writing.
- **Mentorship schemes:** This entails pairing up two people—the "mentee" who has less experience with the more experienced "mentor" to foster the

flow of knowledge from the mentor to the mentee. The mentee often relies on their mentor when dealing with developing work situations.

- **On-the-job training:** This occurs when a new employee takes lessons from their manager or a fellow employee on how to perform their job well. This learning process often involves manual work in a company (e.g. forklifting) but can be extended to other roles as well.
- **E-learning:** E-learning is accomplished through digital resources. It is also known as web-based training and can take the shape of interactive modules or videos.
- **Cross-training:** Here, employees are trained across as many departments within the company as possible. The goal is for staff to become cross-functional, which should improve their performance and level of expertise.

Instructional Design Principles and Processes.

Three out of the four theories of learning we discussed earlier—behavioral, cognitive, and constructivist—form the foundation of instructional design (Mind Tools for Business, 2015). This means that to provide a firm foundation for different lessons in the workplace, the best instructional materials should: provide instruction to the learner, allow for autonomous practice by the learner, and evaluate the learner's performance. This leads us to the concept of training needs.

Training Needs Analysis (Vulpen, 2022)

When a lack of information, skills, or attitudes is the root of the challenge you wish to tackle by providing the training, conducting a training needs analysis ahead of time will help you tackle the issue effectively (Vulpen, 2022). The steps you should think about to figure out your employees' training needs are as follows:

Outline the objectives of the company concerning the training

What are the pain points you need to address and how do they align with the goals of your company? Has your company lost its competitive edge? Is the sales department failing to meet its KPI? Or did senior management identify a skill set that all members of staff must possess?

- **Identify the desired job habit currently lacking**

  Once you know what the pain point is, identifying the job behaviors which will resolve the issue is the next phase of the plan. For instance, if the issue is a lack of technological expertise, would the desired job habit be an engaging PowerPoint presentation by team leaders at every weekly meeting?

- **Identify the knowledge and skills needed**

  The next stage is to deconstruct these high-over actions into the knowledge and skills to show them effectively. It will be simpler to develop training programs that meet these behavioral requirements if you can make these behaviors as specific as possible.

- **Now Create Your Design Template**

  Once you have attended to the questions raised by the previous stages, you can get started with your training design. Communicate the identified desired outcomes to senior management and make a budget. This will help you map out where to begin or end the training process.

What is Process Mapping?

A process map is a tool that graphically depicts the flow of work by identifying the people and things involved in a process, such as when and how to approve employees' leave requests or how to make and transport a product. This can help with employee onboarding, training, assessing how a company can improve, finding process bottlenecks, and enhancing awareness of a process.

To create a process map, it's best to start simple. Which process does your organization use regularly but wish to improve on? Your response should be related to the absence of requests, recruitment, onboarding, or offboarding processes.

Once you've decided, the next thing to do is collect the data you need. You can do this by observing the process (e.g., onboarding) from beginning to end; reviewing current documentation, and meeting with your team and individuals who are most involved in the work one-on-one to figure out the hurdles they face while engaging in that task.

Now that you have the data you need, map out your ideas on how to improve the process from its starting point to the finish line. As you fill in the blanks, pay attention to the places where the key decisions are made and see if you can improve on those as well.

Techniques to Assess Training Program Effectiveness

Knowing how successful your training programs are is a useful metric in assessing whether your company is making good returns on its investment, as well as the areas to improve (Verma, 2022). The Kirkpatrick assessment model (1959) is widely accepted as a way to determine the efficacy of special training schemes. Under the model, the assessment levels include:

- **Reaction**

  This stage assesses how trainees responded to the training, along with its applicability and value. To get the feedback you need, you can use self-evaluation forms or employee polls either before and or after the course. Did they find the program understandable and relevant to their roles? What conclusions did they draw from the training?

- **Learning**

  This level entails the evaluation of the knowledge and skill sets your trainees actually garnered from the program. You can use performance prior to the training to their performance afterward. You can also rely on assessments of applied learning projects, supervisor reports, and feedback to measure this.

- **Behavior**

    This phase involves spotting the effects of the program on the trainee's attitude and conduct at work. You can rely on self-assessment questionnaires, focus groups, on-the-job observations, job KPIs, informal feedback from coworkers, surveys, and/or complaints from customers to measure this. The goal here is to identify how the lessons are being used in the workplace, and whether employees feel comfortable imparting their newly gained skills to their colleagues.

- **Results**

    Last, be sure to assess whether the skills learned in the training result in stronger morale or increases in productivity and sales. Improved corporate outcomes, enhanced efficiency and quality of work, employee satisfaction, higher morale, and a client satisfaction index are all important measures to track here.

Organizational Development Methods.

There are nine main organizational growth techniques (Your Article Library, n.d.), and they are as follows:

- **Survey feedback**

    This is the most well-liked and extensively applied technique for gathering data. With surveys, you can access information relating to working conditions, job standards, working hours, pay, and the overall attitude of employees to the company within which they work.

- **Team building**

    This technique is specially created to improve employees' abilities and inspire them to collaborate. It is a method of organizational development that places a focus on creating teams or working in groups to increase organizational performance.

- **Sensitivity training**

  Employees are asked to interact in groups using this strategy. Sensitivity training attempts to help staff members understand and be more sensitive to the needs of each other so they can all express themselves freely and without fear.

- **Managerial grid**

  Using this technique identifies two major types of behavior—output-oriented and people-oriented. Then both habits are compared and contrasted thoroughly to figure out which works best.

- **Management by objectives (MBO)**

  This is a tool for performance evaluation and review, as well as a method for accomplishing corporate objectives. Here, the organization's goals are identified as clearly as possible to enable team leaders and managers to fully carry out their duties

- **Brainstorming**

  This is a method where five to eight managers get together to think of solutions to issues. Brainstorming fosters creative thinking and is a great way to generate fresh ideas.

- **Process consultation**

  Process consultation is an upgrade over sensitivity training as a method. Here, the consultant or expert offers the participant direction or counsel on how to carefully resolve their issues with someone else.

- **Quality circles**

  In this approach, a group of five to twelve people gathers together once a week during work hours, in the presence of a supervisor, to discuss issues and proffer solutions to management.

- **Transactional analysis**

  Transactional analysis aids in improving interpersonal communication. Although it is an effective tool for organizational development, it also has a variety of other uses, including training, counseling, interpersonal communication, and group dynamics analysis.

- **Task analysis**

  This is the task and competency identification procedure. HR experts examine the task-performance contexts as part of the task analysis process (Assignment Help, n.d.). These requirements cover the tools and working environment, deadlines, safety requirements, and performance expectations. These observations, which are frequently obtained from questionnaires, serve as the foundation for descriptions of work activities or the duties associated with a particular position. The job on which the training will be concentrated would then be determined by this.

Coaching and Mentoring Techniques

Coaching occurs when a more experienced person helps someone less experienced to develop new abilities, increase performance, and improve the quality of their career. Coaching is that it is individualized and is often carried out on a one-on-one basis over a specified time. You also would need to have qualified coaches and a coherent plan of the goals the organization wishes to achieve through coaching.

Mentoring programs that work best are often based on talents and development requirements. Here, less experienced employees are paired with more seasoned workers to improve the former's performance and well-being in the workplace. These programs also have definitive goals, set time commitment minimums, monitor each mentorship closely, and align mentoring to the objectives and strategies of talent management.

As similar as they may seem, coaching differs from mentorship in certain respects. For one, a mentorship program can last for months, while a coaching session could be over in less than 15 minutes. Also, companies can set up mentorship programs a lot quicker than coaching programs because mentors require fewer qualifications than coaches. In coaching sessions, coaches typically ask questions, give the trainee time to reflect, and let them do more of the talking. A mentorship session, in contrast, is likely to feature more lecturing from the mentor. In the end, coaching and mentoring techniques are both about using the expertise of the coach or mentor to help individuals and companies achieve their goals.

Employee Retention Concepts and Applications

The ability of a business to lower the number of employees who leave their position within a time frame, either voluntarily or involuntarily, is known as employee retention (Holliday, 2021). High turnover harms revenue, efficiency, staff satisfaction, and knowledge retention, some of which may have been prevented by earlier management action.

The first step in enhancing employee retention is hiring the best-suited employees. Once a recruit has been selected by the company, orientation and onboarding are crucial to making them feel at home. Other crucial elements of employee retention are opportunities for career growth and recognition for their achievements.

Techniques to Encourage Creativity and Innovation (Stevenson, 2013)

- **Get a structured program to identify and market new or creative services, goods, or concepts**

  You may not realize this, but innovation is constantly taking place within your organization. Without a mechanism to nurture and display that ingenuity, however, much of it can be lost. One way of dealing with this dilemma is to create separate budgets to support innovation ventures outside the company (i.e., to generate ideas or products from non-employees).

- **Make innovation a key capability in your strategy for developing leaders**

  Having creative leaders in your organization encourages dedication to creativity. Leadership and innovation go hand in hand, and so each leader should be accountable for innovation within their department.

- **Establish and advance the organization's innovation-related values**

  If it is explicitly stated that innovation is essential to the company's mission and principles, employees might feel more comfortable taking the steps necessary for successful innovation. The environment for invention would be much improved because of this.

- **Use social media and technology-enabled collaboration tools to spread knowledge**

  You can use forums and other media for collective projects and to spread information to a target demographic. As you implement these changes, keep tabs on innovators in higher education institutions around you. The most successful businesses identify the most talented individuals before their rivals do, often even before they graduate.

Key Takeaways:

- To make the right decisions for your organization, you must fully understand the development programs your company needs to grow while also operating within the confines of the law.
- A training needs analysis refers to the process through which an organization's management team identifies the discrepancy between the knowledge and skills it intends to impart upon employees on the one hand, and the actual knowledge, skills, and attitudes relevant to specific roles or positions within the company.
- A process map is an organizational and management tool that graphically depicts the flow of work by identifying the people and things involved in a process, such as when and how to approve employees' leave requests or how to make and transport a product.
- The effectiveness of a company's training programs can be evaluated through several means, such as post-training tests, one-on-one conversations, feedback from employee surveys, and participant case studies.

Having discussed the various learning schemes and development techniques for your company in this chapter, in the next chapter, you will learn about applying, promoting, and managing employee benefit and compensation programs in accordance with all related federal laws (Study Guide Zone, 2022).

Free Video Offer!

Thank you for purchasing from Hanley Test Preparation! We're honored to help you prepare for your exam. To show our appreciation, we're offering an Exclusive Test Tips Video.

This video includes multiple strategies that will make you successful on your big exam.

All we ask is that you email us your feedback and describe your experience with our product. Amazing, awful, or just so-so. We want to hear what you have to say!

To get your FREE VIDEO, just send us an email at bonusvideo@hanleytestprep.com with **Free Video** in the subject line and the following information in the body of the email:

- The name of the product you purchased
- Your product rating on a scale of 1-5, with 5 being the highest rating.
- Your feedback about the product.

If you have any questions or concerns, please don't hesitate to contact us at support@hanleytestprep.com

Thanks again!

Chapter Five: Total Rewards

The compensation packages an organization provides its employees serve as a tool to draw in and keep talent, improve overall staff well-being, and promote productivity. Let's discuss how you can implement, promote and manage your staff benefits and compensation plans in compliance with the federal rules we discussed in the preceding chapters of this book.

Compensation Policies

Think of a compensation policy as a set of guidelines put out by a company concerning an employee's pay, benefits, and rewards (Chron, 2020). Typical examples of compensation policies include:

- **Employee benefits**

  Companies often specify the criteria for the award of certain benefits or incentives to hardworking employees. For instance, a corporate handbook for a marketing firm could direct that where a worker's overall sales exceed a certain target over a specified time, their hard work may attract a reward from the management.

- **Merit increases**

When deciding on pay or wage increases, organizations that use merit increases to compensate employees rely on data supplied by the assessments of supervisors or team leaders. Where employees achieve the desired performance ratings, merit promotions typically take the form of precise salary increments (e.g., a two percent increase to one's base salary).

- **Pay-for-performance**

This is based on employee performance and so is like a merit increase. The difference is that, unlike merit increases, a pay-for-performance strategy is typically not constrained to certain percentages or contingent on obtaining a certain rating. Employee salaries are raised under pay-for-performance policies when they perform well and help the firm achieve its objectives. For instance, a lawyer may be qualified for a pay increase based on a pay-for-performance compensation scheme if they refer a significant volume of clients or businesses to their law firm.

- **Annual evaluation**

To make sure the business is keeping a competitive edge, human resource professionals should examine compensation plans annually. If the cost-of-living increases in the city within which the company is based, for instance, salaries and earnings should be adjusted to provide as much support as possible to the employees.

- **Budgeting, Payroll, and Accounting Practices for Compensation and Benefits**

Through a variety of techniques (including job order costing and process costing), manufacturing overheads are subsumed into unit product costs in cost accounting (Pearson Education, 2022). The accounting process divides the various components of remuneration into two accounts, typically referred to as indirect or direct labor. These two account types are incorporated into the cost of goods sold.

In the service sector, the cost of the equipment or personnel directly involved in rendering the service is referred to as the cost of the commodities sold. General and administrative expenses typically include extras like the electricity needed to power the devices and workers who are not directly involved in rendering the service. To determine the net profit, the gross profit is often reduced by this overhead or indirect expenses.

Payroll accounting is the relevant accounting field responsible for determining and allocating funds for employee remuneration (Ingram, n.d.). HR professionals often have a variety of management responsibilities, so learning about payroll accounting will help you make sure that your employees get paid on time. According to Ingram (n.d), payroll accounting may seem complicated, but you can still get it right by:

- **Compiling your time logs**

  The first step in payroll accounting is gathering daily and monthly logs of the hours worked by the employees. The time logs for full-time staff would differ from that of part-time employees, so compile your reports carefully. Accountants can accurately record the precise number of hours worked by each employee by assessing the time cards and automated time clocks.

- **Calculation of pay**

  Compensation calculations are sometimes fairly straightforward, and at other times extremely complex. For instance, calculating the negotiated pay rate by the number of hours worked might work for an independent contractor but not a CEO, because accrued incentive bonuses would also need to be considered.

- **Calculation and submission of taxes**

  Both employers and employees must file and submit income taxes, but it is the employer's responsibility to do so. Payroll accountants must determine each employee's income tax liability after determining the gross salary due. The accounting division must then deduct the taxes from the employee's pay and regularly report them to the Internal Revenue Service (IRS).

- **Incentives and paid time off**

  Payroll accountants' jobs grow more challenging if employers provide automated disbursements into 401(k) programs or other investment accounts or
  paid vacation time for workers. An hourly worker on paid leave, for instance,
  may not have a record of the hours they worked while on leave, but would still
  need to be paid for their full work hours. Staff retirement or pension account
  contributions must also be deducted from the employees' salaries and be paid
  out to the business that manages the account.

- **Distribution of pay**

  The last step in payroll accounting is to disburse each employee's net compensation. Depending on staff preferences, salaries can be paid out in cash,
  deposited directly into their bank accounts, or made out in checks and mailed
  to home addresses.

Job analysis and evaluation.

To precisely define the duties, functions, responsibilities, and skill set required
for every role within your organization, you must learn how to identify and fully
assess what each job role entails (Management Study Guide, n.d). A key element
of job analysis is that such an assessment be done of the job or position, rather
than be focused on a specific employee. To conduct such a detailed analysis,
you'd need:

- **The job description:** This refers to a written statement that completely
  describes what a job entails, such as the title of the role, the responsibilities associated with it, the conditions of employment, associated risks, the
  reporting structures, the automated systems and materials to be used, and
  the connection of the job role with other positions within the organization.
- **The job specification:** This document outlines the skills a person is expected to have to do the job effectively. It also includes the level of training, expertise, skill set, talents, and abilities needed to carry out the work.

The results from such a detailed job analysis and evaluation are often realigned to reflect the goals of the organization. As an HR professional, you must interpret the evaluations, note the kinds of adjustments that should be made to the existing roles, and propose them to the management. If requested, you should also offer guidance on how to successfully implement these changes to improve the effectiveness and efficiency of the company.

Job Pricing and Pay Structures

Effective compensation schemes must include salary structures because they ensure that pay packages for subgroups of jobs are both fair and competitive (Davidson, 2021). Now a crucial aspect of job pricing is a pay structure, which is the framework that establishes what an individual gets paid or what a specific job function attracts based on the importance of that job to the company or the efficacy of the employee in that role.

Pay structures are important because not only do they help organizations identify the pay rates for various positions and staff members, but they also create clear payment management procedures to guarantee that employees are continuously compensated fairly for the work they do. This reflects their value to the company and enhances employee satisfaction. According to Davidson (2021), the types of pay structures are:

- **Individual pay rates**

  Under this scheme, each employee within an organization has either a specific hourly or weekly pay rate or an annual income unique to them. This pre-determined pay technique makes it simple and precise to determine employee worth.

- **Individual salary or job ranges**

  This framework differs from individual pay rates in that employees are paid a wage within a pre-defined range rather than merely a fixed salary. As a result, each position or employee has an income salary range associated with it rather than a spot wage.

- **Pay scales with narrow grades**

  Jobs with roughly comparable values are divided into many grades, typically 10 or more, in narrow-graded pay structures. These kinds of organizations are frequently seen in the government sector or in services that were originally very similar. Graduation through each grade is typically accomplished through service increments, which are annual or biannual.

- **Pay schemes with broad grades**

  There are typically six to nine fewer grades in broad-graded pay structures than in narrow-graded structures, and the salary bracket inside this grade is typically wider. There is also an increased opportunity for an employee's compensation to advance farther up the pay grade under this payment structure.

- **Job families**

  Organizations using this structure typically construct many job families for different departments, with distinct pay systems for each family or unit. Because of their adaptability, job families are a great compromise between many other potential compensation systems. They also function effectively as they give businesses both freedom and control while also allowing for employee advancement and transparency.

- **Career families**

  In that there are various families, career families, also known as career-graded structures, are like work-family structures. However, using this strategy, every family uses identical pay scales and grade levels for all levels covered. Instead of placing a greater emphasis on the compensation of job families, the emphasis here is on career planning and advancement.

  Whatever route you take, making sure your team is aware of the proper pay structure can help them fully grasp their place within the company. This is crucial in the long run for increasing productivity and guaranteeing employee satisfaction.

Non-Monetary Compensation.

Any reward provided to a worker in a non-cash format is referred to as non-monetary compensation. This could take the form of a trip awarded to the "Salesperson of the Month," where the prize has value but is not added to the recipient's income. Non-monetary compensation packages make employees feel appreciated and valued by their employers, especially as most of such incentives are geared towards improving the personal lives of staff members (Reynolds, 2019). According to Reynolds (2019), popular instances of non-monetary compensation packages available in modern workplaces today are:

- **Benefits for employees**

  Other benefits that fall under the category of non-financial remuneration, besides health and wellness benefits, are pension funds, tuition assistance, daycare allowances, pet insurance, free or reduced food and drink, and gym memberships. Your company might provide special advantages that are unavailable elsewhere. For instance, you may provide free house cleaning services when employees are at work, on-site salon services on designated days, or a brief leave of absence following the adoption of a new pet.

- **Vacation from work**

  Paid Time Off, like holidays and sick time, is included in the term "time off from work." It also covers unpaid leave, including sabbaticals and leaves required by the Family and Medical Leave Act, as well as time off without pay (FMLA). Conventional maternity and paternity leave and leaves connected to adoptions, and family-related or personal illness are all covered by the FMLA.

- **Opportunities for career development**

  Your organization may have various development possibilities, such as mentoring sessions, job rotations, tuition reimbursement, and other similar programs in place. Encourage all employees to take advantage of such opportunities. These kinds of products are an essential component of your whole incentives strategy because they would enable you to expand your present staff while simultaneously guaranteeing that crucial roles are covered by succession planning.

- **Awards for employee recognition**

  Employee behavior that goes well beyond the usual call of duty is sometimes recognized publicly with the presentation of employee commendation awards. Award categories include staff of the week, month, or year, best team leader, and various forms of peer-to-peer recognition.

- **Work/Life benefits**

  The rules and services your company has implemented to assist employees in better juggling duties at work and home are considered work/life perks. Compressed workweeks, telework options, remote working opportunities, and company services like on-site childcare facilities are a few examples of these advantages.

  Offering even a few of these perks can dramatically increase employee performance and improve your company's total employee value proposition.

Methods to Align and Benchmark Compensation and Benefits

Salary benchmarking in human resources aid businesses in determining how competitively their overall pay is compared to the market. Here is a quick checklist with five stages to use when doing your next benchmarking study (Birches Group, n.d):

- **Start by conducting a high-quality survey**

  You need market information to conduct any benchmarking, and market information typically takes the shape of a survey. This would help you understand how your corporation conducts business at all job levels, beginning with identifying the goals of its positions, figuring out how engaged they are, and looking at how each of its responsibilities is structured and provides services.

- **Compile your grade data**

  Grade information is based on job level and related ranges rather than the real persons who hold those positions. Since grade data includes all positions with the same level of organizational contribution, it is very reliable and a more consistent sign of actual market movement.

- **Be knowledgeable about your market**

  You must choose the survey comparators that apply to your company before you make your assessment. You will need to select a smaller group of comparators that apply to your organization from the larger survey sample.

- **Determine where you fit in the market**

  Determine which tier or fraction of the sample you would like to focus on after you have reduced the choices to your preferred comparators. Competitiveness is not always limited to wages. Talent can also be attracted and retained via allowances and rewards, both financial and non-financial. Your business may decide to pay slightly lower salaries than the market norm while still providing extra advantages. Again, finding that balance depends on the EVP of your organization.

- **Always make use of new data**

  Making sure that you are using the most recent market data is something you might worry about if you are to manage the salary and benefits of your firm. Even businesses with sound compensation plans may find it difficult to remain competitive in the market if they are using stale data.

Benefits Program Policies, Procedures, and Analysis

Every business implements an employee benefits program to satiate and inspire its workforce. Employers offer these perks to employees for a variety of reasons, including medical, leave, amenities, educational, handicap, or health (HR Help Board, n.d). These advantages psychologically increase employees' sense of dependence on the company, which helps the business attract loyal workers. To develop thoughtful benefits plans designed to satisfy both employee demands and employer goals:

- **Determine the organization's benefits, goals, and spending plan**

  Typically, this phase yields a list of specific benefits provided, as well as an outline of the organization's goals to provide benefits that consider the needs of both the employer and the employee. As most firms have financial restrictions when providing benefits to employees, assessing the budget available for spending on benefits is equally crucial.

- **Figure out the needs of the company staff**

  Consider the needs of different employee groups by analyzing the demographics of the current workforce. For instance, younger workers might value increased vacation time, while older workers may value retirement investment plans more.

- **Create a benefits plan program**

  Your organization would need to create a benefits plan design relying on the information gathered from all resources in Step 2 above. Common questions that may come up here include: Can the present policies be altered to save costs without losing their value? Can the company scrap ineffective or under-used benefit programs? Would the company need employees to contribute to the program? Also, what degrees of such contribution would be sufficient?

- **Communication and feedback**

  Even when an employer's efforts are perfectly tailored to meet the needs of its employees, the resultant schemes may be rendered ineffective without communication and useful feedback. If employee feedback was gathered and used in the development of the benefits program, be sure to inform the staff of this and explain how it affected the program's design.

- **Establish a routine evaluation procedure to assess the success of the benefits**

Finally, you must understand that changes in dynamics occur because of shifts in the business environment, the economy, the regulatory environment, and worker demographics. Once a program becomes ineffective, revisit the steps above to set up an updated benefits scheme to replace it.

Key Takeaways:

- The compensation packages an organization provides its employees serve as a tool to draw in and keep talent, improve overall staff well-being, and promote productivity.
- Payroll accounting is the relevant accounting field responsible for determining and allocating funds for employee remuneration.
- Any reward provided to a worker in a non-cash format is referred to as non-monetary compensation. These make employees feel appreciated and valued by their employers, especially as most of such incentives are geared towards improving the personal lives of staff members.
- Salary benchmarking in human resources aids businesses in determining how competitively their overall pay is compared to the market. You must be knowledgeable about this, especially as an HR professional.

In the next chapter, we will discuss the largest aspect of your PHR exam in as much detail as possible. You will learn all about employee labor and relations, including how to implement, manage, and monitor programs and policies that legally enrich the overall employee experience.

Chapter Six: Employee and Labor Relations

Employer-employee relations (ER) is the phrase used to describe the different interactions that exist between the staff and the management of a company or organization (Verlinden, 2022). This term encompasses all aspects of employment relationships, including the legal, practical, economic, and emotional aspects. Let's chat about this more below:

General Employee Relations Activities and Analysis (Verlinden, 2022)

Managing the ER in any organization isn't easy. There could be a variety of concerns being raised daily, and each one may need to be handled appropriately. Employees may, for example, take a lot of unscheduled time off from work, view pornographic content on the company's internet, speak disrespectfully to their boss, argue with coworkers, attend meetings, gossip, exhibit poor personal cleanliness, or break safety regulations. As an HR professional, here are some ways you can handle the relationship between employees and employers in employee relations.

- **Open and sincere communication**

  Create a safe space in your company where no one is reluctant to speak up or raise questions and share administrative updates with your team. Share any changes to company policies with your staff as soon as possible and get their feedback on as many issues as you need to. These are some ways you can build and nurture a foundation of honesty within your organization.

- **Involve your employees in the company's vision**

  Ensure that you regularly share and convey the company's goal and vision. Also, encourage your staff to communicate and share this vision with each other as often as you can. This will give them a sense of belonging and re-inforce the notion that they actively contribute to reaching this common objective.

- **Believe in your team**

  Put differently, avoid micromanaging your staff as much as possible. Let them know they can contact you at any time for further information or if they have questions, and they will always receive a prompt response.

- **Appreciation goes a long way**

  Building excellent employee relations requires showing your concern for them and rewarding them. This can be accomplished by simply sending out emails asking workers to submit their weekly "cheers for peers," which will be shared with everyone else either at the weekly presentation or via email. This will go a long way to encourage positivity and productivity within your company.

- **Invest in your workforce**

  Investing in people is another way to show your care for them and to foster positive employee relations (Petryni, 2019). Fortunately, you can do this in several ways. You can encourage the management to pay for select courses for its staff, or organize relevant training sessions. According to Petryni (2019), the approach you choose may vary depending on the sort of business, sector, and financial constraints of your organization

Applicable Federal Laws and Procedures (Reid, n.d).

The National Labor Relations Act of 1935 (United States Congress), promotes collective bargaining, safeguards the rights of both workers and their employers, and restricts some discriminatory private-sector workplace practices, governs federal labor relations regulations. State labor laws differ, but they cannot go against federal legislation in these matters. Here are some general provisions of the law in relation to specific employment issues:

- **Strikes**

  When an employer violates a collective bargaining agreement, employees go on strike and refuse to come back to work. According to the NLRA and state legislation, this technique is acceptable as long as workers express their complaints to a union leader before stopping work.

- **Union Representation**

  According to federal law, workers are free to form, join, or support a union, discuss job conditions with the union, and work together to improve the workplace.

- **Injustice in the workplace**

  Employers are prohibited from engaging in unfair employment practices that violate the collective bargaining agreement, federal and state labor laws, or both.

Human Relations, Culture, and Values Concepts

The practice of human relations involves educating staff members, attending to their needs, promoting a positive workplace atmosphere, and settling disputes among coworkers or between staff members and management. Underscoring their significance is an appreciation of some of the ways in which human relations can affect the expenses, viability, and long-term economic security of the business.

Understanding and Developing Organizational Culture

According to My Workplace Health (2021), an organization's culture comprises various shared norms, attitudes, beliefs, interpretations, and aspirations that employees use to guide their behavior and problem-solving. Company culture dictates what is expected of employees and the way they'll act. When a company's culture is based on trust, integrity, tolerance, decency, and equality or when it emphasizes things like mental and sociological support, appreciation, and reward, it improves the psychological well-being and safety of the company and its personnel.

Here are some simple ways you can improve your company's culture at work:

- Educate all employees on the principles of effective communication.
- Organize and take part in team-building activities.
- Encourage upper management to launch periodic mentoring programs for new hires and seasoned personnel.
- Explore options for social interaction among the staff. This can be as simple as scheduling group break times a few days in the workweek to socialize with others to promote effective dialogue and connections.
- Maintain open lines of communication among the team's members. Make sure everyone is aware of what each employee brings to the team, and that everyone feels recognized and respected (My Workplace Health, 2021).

Review and Analysis for Assessing Employees' Attitudes, Opinions, and Satisfaction

Just as much as the quality of a company's goods, services, and prices can affect its financial performance, employee attitudes can directly affect a company as well (McQuerrey, n.d). The reason for this is simple: customers, coworkers, and bosses alike can all tell when an employee has a poor attitude or executes their assigned tasks poorly.

As a PHR, part of your responsibility to your organization is assessing and nipping such situations in the bud. Fortunately, you can ask a series of open-ended questions to workers in various contexts to gauge how your company's workers feel about their jobs, the workplace, and their direct managers. According to McQuerry (n.d), the steps to accomplish this are as follows:

- Create a questionnaire for employees as an essay asking them to discuss problems at work. Avoid yes or no answer questions because these would limit their feedback to you.
- Convene a focus group with both employees and their supervisors in a roundtable fashion and ask them to rate various areas of business operations. Make them feel safe, and encourage them to expound on their replies rather than just answering yes or no during the session. Ensure that you don't get offended by their responses.
- Alternatively, you can hold one-on-one interviews about what changes they would suggest to the organization or to each of their specific departments.
- Throughout the year, provide a suggestion box and invite staff to share anonymously any difficulties, challenges, or those concerns they feel awkward writing about or discussing in a group. This can also be a great way for them to raise complaints about improper conduct or the discriminatory acts they face.

Inclusion and diversity

The concepts of inclusion and diversity, while fairly recent, have permeated every aspect of our lives today. In the workplace, these principles simply posit that employees should be as diverse as possible or differ in terms of gender, color, age, and other personal characteristics. As an HR professional, your role in an inclusive or diverse workplace is to offer diversity, sensitivity, and cultural awareness training programs in order to reap the benefits of diversity. This is important because the more diverse a workforce is, the higher chances of friction arising from communication limitations. Both formal and casual communication should be encouraged as much as possible, and this is where those training programs can help.

Record-keeping requirements

A company's document and information lifecycle, from the time it is generated or collected until it is archived for record purposes or deleted, is governed by the Fair Labor Standards Act (United States Congress, 1938).

Under this Act, employers are required to maintain all payroll data, as well as sales and purchase records, for a minimum of three years. Also, employers are mandated to maintain and secure the information they collected from their employees at the onset of the recruitment process, throughout the duration of the employment contract, and after its termination. Your responsibilities as a PHR involve ensuring that all these provisions are strictly adhered to.

Occupational Injury and Illness Prevention Techniques

Accidents are unforeseen events that cause damage to property, disease, death, and lost productivity. They may not be totally prevented, but they can be reduced with the right plans, preparations, and actions (Ohio State University, n.d). These include:

- **Understanding the risks**

  Examine your surroundings. Locate any potential dangers in the workplace by looking around. Find strategies to lessen or get rid of dangers and put them into practice. Report dangerous areas or behaviors. Be prepared for the weather.

- **Establish a secure workspace**

  Maintain a tidy workplace. The office's layout needs to have sufficient exit routes and be clear of waste. Company vehicles should be checked both before and after use.

- **Use safe lifting methods**

  Follow these secure lifting procedures: Lift with strength, keep the load close, adopt a staggered posture, and avoid twisting while doing so. Body mechanics instruction can lower strain injuries and keep workers secure while lifting and moving.

- **Equipment for personal protection**

  Injury risk can be significantly decreased by providing and training your staff in using the best personal protective equipment (PPE) they need to execute their tasks. Equipment like earplugs, safety helmets, protective goggles, hard hats, air-purifying protective suits, and safety boots are good examples of PPE.

- **Consistent communication**

  Always keep the managers, supervisors, and team leaders informed of any new potential risk factors in your workplace. The more knowledgeable everyone is about these risks, the more cautious they would be and the lesser the chances of work accidents happening.

Workplace Safety and Security Risks

One of the many important factors that a person considers at a company before joining the organization is security. Your organization has a legal responsibility to give its employees a safe working environment and, as the HR professional, it is your duty to ensure that this is done.

Emergency Response and Disaster Recovery Process

A Disaster Recovery Plan (DRP) is a crucial management tool that aids in a company's disaster recovery (SIB Blog. (2022). Senior staff members typically make up DRP teams, which are carefully chosen from several departments. Disaster Recovery Planning mostly relies on the Human Resource division. Within this context, some of the HR functions include:

- Teaching employees the DRP-compliant emergency response procedures.
- Providing for staff members' families where an evacuation may be required in regions that are prone to natural disasters. This will lessen concerns among the workers.
- Establishing and maintaining channels of contact with all stakeholders, as well as with emergency services.
- Acting as the single point of contact for all information relating to the disaster to maintain accuracy and focus.
- Keeping track of every worker going on an assignment away from the office.

Internal Investigation Techniques.

In human interaction within a company, there may be complaints that would require further investigation. The Human Resources department handles such internal investigations, especially managing employee behavior within the organization. According to Cosentino (n.d), you can effectively conduct such investigations in the following steps:

- **Start the process as quickly as possible**

  As an HR professional who understands the importance of employee satisfaction, respond right away to protect the accuser or the complainant, depending on the specifics of the accusation. For instance, if the parties to the complaint work closely together, you might need to separate them.

- **Select the investigator and decision-maker**

  A legal counsel or a member of the HR department's internal staff may serve in this capacity, but they cannot be connected to either the complainant or the accused. To establish the facts of what occurred, it is also crucial to ensure that the investigator works impartially and fairly.

- **Create an investigation plan**

  To determine whether the complaint is true, the appointed investigator must first draft an investigative strategy. As a PHR, it's your job to ensure that the outline produced is properly done. Also, maintaining anonymity is crucial when carrying out a workplace investigation.

- **Interviews and inquisitions**

  To gain the pertinent facts and specifics regarding the complaints, ensure that the investigator prepares their target interview questions in advance. You can request written statements from the people involved besides interviewing to get their perspectives on the matter.

- **Detailed reports of the results of the investigations**

  Each phase of the investigation should be properly documented, not just for transparency, but also because a holistic review of all details would help the decision-makers resolve the complaint. It's crucial to remember that the investigator would only make recommendations based on their findings, not final decisions.

- **Share the investigation's findings**

  The investigator will share the report with the decision-maker and the affected parties as soon as it is finished. Once this is done, the investigator's part in the process ends. Instead, based on the report, the decision-maker will choose what action has to be taken and whether disciplinary action is required. If the decision subsequently made differs from the investigator's recommendation, be sure to provide the justifications for such decisions in the report as an appendix.

- **Decide how to proceed**

Finally, at the end of the process, come up with creative ways to boost the morale of your employees. You can, for instance, encourage your staff to view the investigation as a chance to provide goal-focused feedback or constructive criticisms that would improve the overall performance of your team.

Data Privacy and Security

According to the Privacy Research Team (2022), employers must ensure that the data of their employees is protected at all times. Information like name, address, social security number, bank account information, etc., are examples of personal data. Any organization's HR department needs to be aware of these regulations and help the company discharge its obligations throughout the duration of an employment contract.

For instance, during the hiring process, employers are mandated by law to inform all job candidates of the kinds of personal information they will need from them and how it will be used. The information gathered must be relevant to the duties of the position being sought after.

Next, during employment, the employer should only collect, handle, and keep employee data that is required, pertinent, and reasonable to whatever role they play in the employment relationship. Employers are also required to take reasonable and suitable security precautions to safeguard the information of their employees. In addition, they must always update all affected employees and/or regulatory authorities as soon as possible if employees' data is accessed, obtained, or compromised in any security breach.

Finally, at the termination of the employment contract, the law dictates that the personal information of all ex-employees must be destroyed if they are no longer required. If an employer wants to keep an employee's information for future employment, they must first get the employee's permission to do so. Former employees may also see the information that an employer has about them.

The Collective Bargaining Process

The process through which an organization and its workers' union negotiate and bargain for the interest of both the company and all employees is referred to as collective bargaining (Open Libraries, n.d). The primary aim here is for management and the union to come to a contract agreement that can be implemented for a predetermined time. To be lawful, collective bargaining must always be conducted in good faith.

The process of collective bargaining may take some time, especially because it is initiated by the compilation of data and a review of the existing employment contract. Afterward, the parties would then set up deadlines for the negotiations, announce their demands, and bargain over those demands. A negotiation deadlock happens when parties cannot agree on a healthy compromise.

While unfair labor practices are prohibited by law, an economic strike often happens during those bargaining talks. Employees may also miss work on grounds of illness while negotiations are ongoing. These are often tactics used to persuade the opposing party to accept the terms of collective bargaining.

Performance Management Process

Through constant communication and engagement between staff and management, performance management aims to ensure that the company's key goals are realized (Lalwani, 2020). According to Lalwani (2020), performance management comprises the following five essential steps:

- **Organizing**

  Setting and discussing goals with staff is part of this step. These objectives should be clearly stated from the time an individual is hired, even if they had been stated in the job description to draw in quality applicants.

- **Observing**

  Managers must monitor how their team members are doing in their roles.

You can monitor the performance of your team in real-time and adjust your strategy as needed with the proper performance management software relevant to your industry.

- **Developing**

  You can use the information gathered during the monitoring or observation phase to help your employees perform better. For instance, to boost performance or maintain excellence, it might be necessary to recommend refresher courses or change the policies for employee growth.

- **Evaluation**

  To assess the performance of employees and make adjustments as necessary, performance ratings are practically indispensable. These evaluations can be given by both peers and team leaders alike.

- **Rewarding**

  Always remember that to effectively manage performance and increase employee engagement, it is crucial to recognize and reward excellent performance.

Termination Approaches.

Everyone taking part in the employee termination process goes through a hard moment. As an HR professional, you must be involved in the process to guarantee the greatest results (Human Resources MBA, n.d.). Here are a few appropriate ways your input would help smoothen out the process:

- **Contributing to the decision**

  In small businesses where the human resources manager may also play other duties, this is most likely to occur.

- **Remittance of salary or severance packages**

  Human resources departments often handle all payroll issues, and should ensure that a terminated employee receives payment for all work performed until their dismissal. Where there are severance packages involved, they should also ensure that this is resolved amicably.

- **Ensuring that due process is followed**

  Making sure that corporate policy is properly followed throughout the termination process is one of the most important duties that HR departments should perform. In terms of internal corporate policy, this is done to maintain uniformity and fairness.

- **Hiring legal counsel where required**

  Finally, a terminated employee who feels wronged may file a claim for wrongful termination against the corporation. As an HR professional, part of your responsibilities in any such situation would be to liaise with supervisors and consult external legal counsel to ensure a fair resolution of the issues raised.

Key Takeaways:

- Employer-employee relations (ER) is the phrase used to describe the different interactions that exist between the staff and the management of a company or organization. This term encompasses all aspects of employment relationships, including the legal, practical, economic, and emotional aspects.

- The practice of human relations involves educating staff members, attending to their needs, promoting a positive workplace atmosphere, and settling disputes among coworkers or between staff members and management.

- As an HR professional, your role in an inclusive or diverse workplace means you would organize and offer diversity, sensitivity, and cultural awareness training programs to reap the benefits of diversity.

- Everyone taking part in the employee termination process goes through a tough moment. As an HR professional, you must be involved in the process to guarantee the greatest results.

We have discussed the different aspects of the PHR exam as extensively as possible until this point. In the next two chapters, you will be provided a full-length practice test, complete with detailed answers and writing instructions. So grab your writing materials and let us begin.

Chapter Seven: Full-Length Practice Test #1

Instructions

These questions below have been included to prepare you for the PHR exam, and test your knowledge of the major test areas we've already discussed in the preceding chapters of this book. Check the answers for this practice test in the answer key section (below the test) to get immediate feedback. You can retake this test as many times as you'd like until your responses improve. While there are 175 questions, the first 25 questions are pretest questions and your answers to them would not count towards the determination of your final test score. (Source: HRCI Practice Exam, 2010).

Total exam time: three hours.

1. Human Resource departments serve a strategic role in most organizations because:

   A. Today's organizations are instituting HR practices aimed at gaining a competitive advantage through their employees.
   B. Today's organizations are increasingly engaged in downsizing and layoff processes.
   C. Globalization has reduced competition.
   D. The workforce is becoming less diverse.

2. Human Resources departments support organizational strategy implementation in all the following ways EXCEPT:

   A. Restructuring efforts.
   B. Instituting incentive plans, such as pay-for-performance plans.
   C. Developing and marketing the organization' s products and services.
   D. Retraining employees for redesigned work.

3. Title VII of the 1964 Civil Rights Act prohibits employment discrimination based on

   A. Race, color, or ethnic background.
   B. Race, religion, or sexual orientation.
   C. Race, color, religion, sex, or national origin.
   D. Race, gender, or religion.

4. Strategic organizational issues related to employee compensation include all the following EXCEPT:

   A. Whether to emphasize seniority or performance.
   B. How to handle salary compression.
   C. Whether employees should be paid weekly, biweekly, or monthly.
   D. Who should distribute paychecks to employees.

5. A specialized approach to organizational change in which the employees themselves formulate the change that is required and implement it, often with the help of a trained consultant, is:

   A. Organizational development.
   B. Skills training.
   C. Employee orientation.
   D. Sensitivity training.

6. Human Resource professionals need to understand the relationship between employee training and organizational strategy because:

   A. Training always results in improved performance.

B. HR departments are responsible for delivering employee training.
C. Training is often part of managerial efforts to renew or reinvent the organization so that it can meet a strategic challenge.
D. Employees generally enjoy training programs.

7. An organizational development technique that aims to improve the performance and interaction within a specific group of employees is:

A. Team building.
B. Technical skills training.
C. Human factors engineering.
D. Survey research.

8. The U.S. Department of Commerce created The Malcolm Baldridge Award to:

A. Reward organizations for commitment to equal employment opportunity.
B. Recognize small businesses that have sustained profitability during difficult times.
C. Recognize organizational quality efforts.
D. Reward organizations for efforts in community service.

9. Distinguishing characteristics of self-directed teams include all the following EXCEPT:

A. Strong managerial leadership.
B. Naturally interdependent tasks.
C. Enriched jobs.
D. Employee empowerment.

10. Training for ISO 9000 typically covers all the following EXCEPT:

A. The quality-related vocabulary associated with ISO 9000.
B. Requirements regarding record keeping.
C. The measurements embedded in each ISO 9000 section.
D. Specific penalties for employees who fail ISO 9000 standards.

11. HR-related guidelines for building effective self-directed teams include:

    A. Designate a strong leader as manager of the team.
    B. Eliminate cross-training so that workers can concentrate on their jobs.
    C. Provide extensive training so that team members have the skills needed to do their jobs.
    D. Assigning employees who dislike teams to work together as a team to overcome their resistance.

12. Human Resources departments can contribute significantly to business process re-engineering by:

    A. Strengthening the top-down communication process.
    B. Moving from teams to functional departments.
    C. Eliminating the distractions of cross-training.
    D. Redesigning work with a focus on multitasked, enriched, generalist work.

13. A work redesign plan whereby employees build their workday around a core of midday hours is:

    A. A compressed work week.
    B. Job sharing.
    C. Flextime.
    D. Telecommuting.

14. Which of the following is true regarding flexible work arrangements?

    A. Job sharing and work sharing are different terms for the same process.
    B. Compressed work weeks are suitable for organizations that offer services continuously, 24 hours a day.
    C. Most firms using flexible work arrangements give employees broad freedom regarding the hours they work.
    D. Flextime arrangements have been most successful in factory jobs.

15. A comprehensive process to determine the effectiveness of a firm's HR policies and procedures would most likely include:

    A. An HR audit.
    B. Comparison of the firm's compensation practices with peer firms.
    C. An analysis of turnover and absenteeism in the HR department.
    D. A re-design of the performance appraisal process.

16. With regard to global HR management, HR practitioners should note that:

    A. Research shows that a significant number of employees will leave the firm within two years of returning home after an international assignment.
    B. Repatriation agreements are considered ineffective processes in today's international organizations.
    C. Labor strikes occur frequently in European countries.
    D. The adjustment of the employee's spouse and family to the new country is rarely a significant factor in employee performance.

17. Current global pressures that affect HR strategic management include all the following EXCEPT:

    A. Employee skills deployment to the appropriate location.
    B. Knowledge dissemination throughout the organization.
    C. Identifying and developing employee talent globally.
    D. Stressing to employees that cultures are the same around the world.

18. The management functions of most HR departments include:

    A. Both line and staff responsibilities.
    B. Staff responsibilities but not line responsibilities.
    C. Line responsibilities but not staff responsibilities.
    D. Neither line nor staff responsibilities.

19. Technological changes in the workplace have influenced the practice of HR management because:

    A. Employees need less training when organizations use technology.
    B. Technological changes have changed the nature of work.
    C. Organizational spending on technology has reduced the funds available for HR functions.
    D. As technology advances, firms become less competitive.

20. An important workforce demographic consideration for HR professionals is that:

    A. The workforce has become less diverse in recent years.
    B. The average age of the labor force is declining.
    C. Older workers are more likely to remain in the workforce past the age of 65.
    D. Diversity initiatives are no longer needed in most organizations.

21. HR departments contribute a unique perspective to the organizational strategic planning process because:

    A. HR offers training programs in the strategic planning process.
    B. HR handles strategy implementation regarding restructuring and organizational development.
    C. HR maintains records of employee performance.
    D. HR is responsible for compensation surveys.

22. Outsourcing of HR functions is a valuable organizational strategy because this strategy:

    A. Reduces costs.
    B. Increases employee commitment to the organization.
    C. Decreases turnover and absenteeism.
    D. Offers employees improved benefits packages.

23. As an organizational technology tool, HR portals are used to:

    A. Provide employees with a single access point or gateway to organizational HR information.
    B. Allow employees to communicate with each other via electronic mail.
    C. Streamline the performance appraisal process.
    D. Minimize union organizing activity.

24. A key determinant of organizational success in a welfare-to-work program is:

    A. Offering salaries that are higher than industry standards.
    B. Pre-employment training initiatives, including new employee counseling and basic skills training.
    C. Hiring only those who speak English as their native language.
    D. Hiring only relatives of current employees.

25. Organizational efforts to eliminate the present effects of past discriminatory practices are collectively known as:

    A. Affirmative action.
    B. Equal employment opportunity.
    C. Reverse discrimination.
    D. Compliance strategies.

26. Which of the following actions would likely be deemed discriminatory?

    A. Pay differences between men and women based on seniority.
    B. Replacing a worker aged 60 with a worker aged 42.
    C. Refusing to hire women in a private for-profit business with eight male employees.
    D. Requiring disabled workers to perform the essential functions of the job for which they were hired.

27. Title VII of the Civil Rights Act of 1964 prohibits employment discrimination based on:

   A. Race, color, religion, sex, or national origin.
   B. Race, religion, or gender.
   C. Appearance, race, color, or sex.
   D. Race, religion, color, sexual orientation, or gender.

28. A major provision of the Civil Rights Act of 1991 is that:

   A. It limits compensatory and punitive damages for employers found liable for discriminatory practices.
   B. It placed the burden of proof back on employers and permitted the awarding of compensatory and punitive damages.
   C. It permits the awarding of compensatory damages but not punitive damages.
   D. It permits the awarding of punitive damages but not compensatory damages.

29. A basic provision of the Americans with Disabilities Act is that employers must:

   A. Hire disabled individuals and then lower performance standards so that the disabled will not be adversely affected by their disability.
   B. Make reasonable accommodations for disabled workers, even if doing so results in undue hardship to the company.
   C. Provide increased benefits to disabled workers, based on the extent of their disability.
   D. Not discriminate against individuals who can perform the essential functions of a job, with or without reasonable accommodation.

30. The first step in the job analysis process entails:

   A. Deciding how the organization will use the information collected.
   B. Writing new job descriptions for all current employees.
   C. Comparing old job descriptions with new job specifications.
   D. Replacing job descriptions with job specifications.

31. A written statement that describes the activities and responsibilities of a job, as well as important features such as working conditions and safety hazards, is a:

A. Job analysis.
B. Job specification.
C. Job description.
D. Workforce warning and retraining notification statement.

32. The final step in a job analysis process is:

A. Verify the analysis data with the worker performing the job and his or her immediate supervisor.
B. Develop a job description and job specification.
C. Decide how the analysis information will be used.
D. Collect the job analysis data.

33. Designing job specifications based on statistical analysis:

A. Is a quick, low-cost approach to the process.
B. Is more defensible than a managerial judgment approach.
C. Is helpful in recruitment, but not a good predictor of employee performance.
D. Is illegal under Title VII of the Civil Rights Act of 1964.

34. Which of the following is true with regard to predicting organizational employment needs?

A. Trend analysis examines future practices to predict future needs.
B. Computerized methods of employment forecasting are useful in small organizations but ineffective in large organizations.
C. Ratio analysis examines the relationship between a causal factor (such as sales volume) and the number of employees needed.
D. Predictions based on the scatter plot approach are often inaccurate.

35.   Using a yield pyramid is most helpful in:

    A. The recruiting process.
    B. The performance appraisal process.
    C. The employee discipline process.
    D. The interviewing process.

36.   Which of the following would likely be the least effective method of recruiting internal job candidates?

    A. Posting information on organizational bulletin boards.
    B. Examining HR records of current employees.
    C. Advertising in national newspapers and journals.
    D. Consulting organizational skills banks.

37.   The contemporary contingent workforce

    A. Is generally limited to clerical or maintenance staff.
    B. Is declining as firms continue to outsource.
    C. Is made up of workers who do not have permanent jobs.
    D. Is considered a staffing alternative of last resort.

38.   In the selection process, test validity refers to:

    A. The accuracy with which the test measures what it purports to measure nor fulfills the function it was designed to fill.
    B. The consistency of scores obtained by the same person when retested with the same or equivalent tests.
    C. The number of criteria included in the test.
    D. The range of scores possible on the test.

39.   With regard to Equal Employment Opportunity aspects of testing in the selection process:

    A. If tests are valid, the tests need not show a relationship to job performance.
    B. Employers should avoid testing, as testing has been shown to violate the rights of protected classes.

C. Testing always results in adverse impact.

D. Employers must be able to prove the relationship between performance on the test and performance on the job.

40. An employer who wants to measure job performance directly rather than indirectly would likely use which of the following testing processes?

   A. An intelligence test.
   B. A test of manual dexterity.
   C. A work sample test.
   D. A personality test.

41. An employer who wishes to hire a recent immigrant should note the following related to U.S. immigration law:

   A. A person must be a U.S. citizen or have started the naturalization process, to be lawfully employed in the U.S.
   B. New employees must sign the I-9 verification form to certify that they are eligible for employment in the U.S.
   C. EEOC regulations do not apply to foreign-born workers.
   D. To be eligible for employment, immigrants must sign an oath of allegiance to the U.S.

42. A primary advantage of unstructured versus structured interviewing techniques is that:

   A. Unstructured interviews take less time.
   B. In an unstructured interview, the interviewer can ask follow-up questions and pursue points of interest as they develop.
   C. Unstructured interviews comply with EEOC regulations, whereas structured interviews are not.
   D. Unstructured interviews are more cost-effective.

43. Which of the following types of interviews are the most reliable and valid?

   A. Unstructured interviews.
   B. Structured interviews.

C. Stress interviews.

D. Panel interviews.

44. Factors that can undermine the usefulness of an interview include all the following except:

A. Not knowing the requirements of the job.

B. Not knowing the job candidate.

C. Being under pressure to hire.

D. The effect of the order in which candidates were interviewed.

45. Organizations wishing to ensure a suitable supply of employees for current and future senior or key jobs should consider implementing:

A. Succession planning.

B. Work-life initiatives.

C. Higher compensation rates.

D. A stress interviewing process.

46. HR professionals should know the following about unemployment insurance benefits:

A. Benefits are not paid unless the employee submits to an exit interview.

B. Firms are required to pay benefits only for employees dismissed through no fault of their own.

C. Unemployment insurance benefits are not available to exempt employees.

D. In most cases, unemployment insurance benefits expire in eight weeks.

47. 47. The primary purpose of new employee orientation is to:

A. Help the new employee feel comfortable in the organization.

B. Reduce employee lawsuits.

C. Provide new employees with basic information so that they can perform their jobs satisfactorily.

D. Reduce turnover and absenteeism.

48. The best medium for recruiting blue-collar and entry-level workers is generally:

A. The local newspaper.
B. Nationally distributed newspapers.
C. Trade journals.
D. The Internet.

49. Employers may wish to use employment agencies in the recruiting process because:

A. It is generally less expensive to outsource recruiting than to do it in-house.
B. Agencies can generally fill a particular opening more quickly than in-house HR departments.
C. Agencies almost always provide higher quality candidates than those recruited by HR departments.
D. Candidates, not the prospective employer, pay the agency's fees.

50. Regarding flexible work arrangements such as compressed work week programs and flextime, HR professionals should note the research that indicates:

A. Flexible work schedules have a positive effect on employee productivity, but may increase worker fatigue.
B. In shift work, a change to 12-hour shifts from 8-hour shifts creates more confusion, since there are fewer shift changes.
C. Flexible schedules are likely to increase absenteeism.
D. As programs become more flexible, they have more advantages and fewer disadvantages.

51. Which of the following job analysis methods offers the most quantifiable measures of job duties?

A. Observation.
B. The Position Analysis Questionnaire.
C. A participant diary.
D. An interview.

52. Which of the following job analysis methods quantifies job duties in the three specific areas of data, people, and things?

    A. The Department of Labor job analysis procedure.
    B. The Position Analysis Questionnaire.
    C. An unstructured interview.
    D. A participant diary.

53. An advantage of job analysis methods that use quantitative measures is that:

    A. HR professionals can group together, and assign similar pay to, all jobs with similar scores, even if the jobs are very different.
    B. Methods that use quantitative measures are much less expensive than non-quantitative methods.
    C. Quantitative measures never change, unlike non-quantitative measures.
    D. It is much easier to plan employee training programs if quantitative measures are used.

54. HR professionals should use multiple sources of information when conducting job analysis because:

    A. Using only one source of information may lead to inaccurate conclusions.
    B. It is less expensive to use multiple sources.
    C. Quantifiable information is frequently erroneous.
    D. It is less time-consuming to use multiple sources.

55. Regarding writing job specifications, HR professionals should know that:

    A. Identifying the specifications for trained workers is much more complex than for untrained workers.
    B. Identifying the specifications for untrained workers is much more complex than for trained workers.
    C. Job specifications are not needed for trained workers.
    D. Job specifications are not needed for untrained workers.

56. HR professionals who base job specifications on statistical analysis rather than judgment should note that:

   A. Basing job specifications on statistical analysis is a more defensible approach.
   B. Basing job specifications on judgment is a more defensible approach.
   C. Neither approach is defensible.
   D. Statistical analysis involves an examination of qualitative, rather than quantitative, data.

57. Systematically moving workers from one job to another is known as:

   A. Job enlargement.
   B. Job enrichment.
   C. Job rotation.
   D. Dejobbing.

58. Which of the following would be LEAST likely used when selecting staff for assignments outside the U.S.?

   A. An adaptability screening test.
   B. The Overseas Assignment Inventory.
   C. A test of foreign language speaking ability.
   D. An occupational preferences test.

59. An HR staffing plan would likely include all the following EXCEPT:

   A. Projected turnover.
   B. Employee skills and quality.
   C. Financial resources available to the HR department.
   D. An analysis of the causes of absenteeism in the organization.

60. Personnel replacement charts are primarily used for:

   A. Forecasting the supply of internal job candidates.
   B. Forecasting the supply of external job candidates.
   C. Writing job descriptions.
   D. Conducting exit interviews.

61. Which of the following tests would likely be considered the MOST valid in terms of job relatedness?

    A. A mathematics test for factory workers.
    B. A manual dexterity test for insurance sales staff.
    C. A typing test for medical transcriptionists.
    D. A management assessment center for data processors.

62. If an employment selection test constitutes a fair sample of the duties of the job, the test has what kind of validity?

    A. Content validity.
    B. Criterion validity.
    C. Construct validity.
    D. Position validity.

63. The process of forecasting the supply of internal job candidates would be LEAST likely to use which of the following:

    A. Qualifications inventories.
    B. Personnel replacement charts.
    C. Position replacement cards.
    D. Exit interviews.

64. A hospital that needs to recruit newly licensed physical therapists would probably be most successful by targeting its recruiting efforts toward:

    A. Fitness centers.
    B. University physical therapy departments.
    C. Internal job postings.
    D. Local physicians.

65. Which of the following recruiting advertisements would likely be deemed in violation of EEO regulations?

    A. "Experienced housekeeper wanted"
    B. "Nursery school seeks mature child care worker"
    C. "Young man needed for insurance sales position"

D. "Female model needed for hosiery manufacturer"

66.   Regarding employee recruiting, the term "head hunter" refers to:

A. Candidates who are over-qualified for the job.
B. Executive recruiters.
C. Former employees who wish to return to the company.
D. Entry-level candidates who demand large salaries.

67.   Using the Internet in the recruiting process would be most useful when the company is attempting to recruit:

A. Laborers.
B. Data processors.
C. Mail clerks.
D. Bookkeepers.

68.   Federal laws that affect employment references include all the following except:

A. The Privacy Act of 1974.
B. The Fair Credit Reporting Act of 1970.
C. The Family Education Rights and Privacy Act of 1974.
D. The Age Discrimination in Employment Act of 1967.

69.   The most widely used HR selection tool is:

A. The interview.
B. Cognitive testing.
C. The assessment center.
D. Motor skills testing.

70.   If a company wishes to measure a job candidate's stability, introversion, and motivation, it would be most likely to use which of the following selection tests:

A. Intelligence tests.

B. Honesty tests.

C. Personality tests.

D. Handwriting analysis.

71. The Thematic Apperception Test, the Wonderlic Personal Characteristics Test, and the Minnesota Multiphasic Inventory are examples of:

   A. Manual dexterity tests.

   B. Personality tests.

   C. Intelligence tests.

   D. Work sample tests.

72. Using a structured interviewing technique would likely achieve all the following EXCEPT:

   A. Increased consistency across candidates.

   B. Reduced subjectivity on the part of the interviewer.

   C. Enhanced job relatedness.

   D. More opportunities to explore areas as they arise during the interview.

73. A stress interview technique would be most appropriate for which of the following jobs?

   A. An executive chef.

   B. A secretary.

   C. A paralegal.

   D. An air traffic controller.

74. A well-designed new employee orientation program is likely to accomplish all the following EXCEPT:

   A. Fewer mistakes by the new employee.

   B. An appreciation of the company's core values.

   C. An understanding of policies and procedures.

   D. Faster advancement in the organization for the new employee.

75. The requirement that employment selection tests must be job-related was established by which Supreme Court case?

    A. Griggs v. Duke Power Company.
    B. Price Waterhouse v. Hopkins.
    C. Meritor Savings Bank v. Vinson.
    D. Wards Cove Packing Company v. Atonio.

76. Employees who are not citizens of the countries in which they are working are called:

    A. Expatriates.
    B. Home-country nationals.
    C. Third-country nationals.
    D. Naturalized citizens.

77. HR professionals can best promote transferability of training by:

    A. Using well-prepared speakers for training programs.
    B. Maximizing the similarity between the training situation and the work situation.
    C. Using technology in the delivery of training programs.
    D. Offering incentives to employees who attend training programs.

78. The most appropriate method of assessing the training needs of new employees is:

    A. Task analysis.
    B. Performance analysis.
    C. Cognitive analysis.
    D. Psychological analysis.

79. Verifying that there is an employee performance deficiency and determining if training is an appropriate solution is:

    A. Task analysis.
    B. Performance analysis.

C. Behavioral analysis.

D. Deficiency analysis.

80. Methods of determining employee training needs include all the following EXCEPT:

    A. Reviewing performance appraisals.
    B. Analyzing customer complaints.
    C. Interviewing employees and supervisors.
    D. Examining compensation records.

81. An example of a specific performance deficiency amenable to employee training is:

    A. "John has a poor attitude toward his job."
    B. "Mary is always complaining about her co-workers in the department."
    C. "Expectations for sales staff are eight new contacts per week, but Jim averages only two."
    D. "Despite repeated reprimands, Jennifer just isn't working hard enough at her job."

82. In developing employee training programs, HR professionals should first:

    A. Distinguish between "can't do" and "won't do" in terms of employee performance.
    B. Inventory the organization's supply of training programs to determine which program to present.
    C. Match the appropriate employee groups with the appropriate training program.
    D. Examine the organization's compensation structure to determine the cause of the performance problem.

83. Performance task analysis would likely include all the following EXCEPT:

    A. Quality of the performance.
    B. Conditions under which the task is performed.
    C. When and how often the task is performed.

D. Compensation paid for performing the task.

84.   The first step in the delivery of on-the-job training is:

A. Demonstrate the task for the learner.
B. Prepare the learner for the training.
C. Ask the learner to perform the task.
D. Correct the employee as needed during the performance of the task.

85.   A step-by-step self-learning method that consists of presenting the information, allowing a response, and providing feedback on the response is:

A. Programmed training.
B. On-the-job training.
C. Apprenticeship training.
D. Simulated training.

86.   The main advantage of programmed training over other training methods is that:

A. Programmed training allows trainees to learn much more about the tasks to be performed.
B. It is easier to measure performance improvement with programmed training.
C. Programmed training reduces training time.
D. Programmed training is the least expensive training method.

87.   Specific training needs of employees on international assignments include:

A. Task analysis training.
B. Cultural differences awareness.
C. Manual dexterity enhancement.
D. Cognitive skills training

88.   The Human Resource department's contributions to an organizational re-engineering process would likely include all the following EXCEPT:

    A. Building employee commitment to the process.
    B. Re-formulating the organization's mission and goals.
    C. Redesigning work processes.
    D. Redesigning compensation strategies.

89.   The effectiveness of an employee training program would best be determined by:

    A. Measuring employee performance before and after the training was provided.
    B. Comments from supervisors regarding the content of the training program.
    C. The number of employees who attended the training program.
    D. Determining employee reaction to the training program.

90.   The first step in an effective performance appraisal process is to:

    A. Define the job being appraised.
    B. Measure the employee's performance on job tasks.
    C. Give feedback to the employee about job performance.
    D. Observe the employee's on-the-job behaviors.

91.   The simplest and most widely used technique for appraising performance is:

    A. The paired comparison method.
    B. The graphic rating scale.
    C. Management by objectives.
    D. The forced distribution method.

92. The most effective way to evaluate performance management programs is to:

   A. Quantify performance expectations, deliver the program, and assess differences in performance before and after the program.
   B. Compare the costs of such programs and select the one that is most cost-effective.
   C. Survey supervisors by using a questionnaire, survey, or another quantitative analysis tool.
   D. Survey customers for their input on employee performance improvement.

93. Organizations can promote employee involvement in the performance appraisal process by using which of the following strategies?

   A. Peer performance appraisal and self-appraisal.
   B. Customer comment forms.
   C. Basing compensation decisions on performance ratings.
   D. Using job enrichment for all employees.

94. A major implication of current career development approaches is that:

   A. Companies will need to increase spending on career development programs.
   B. HR development activities serve not only the company's needs but also the needs of individual employees.
   C. Companies should not provide career development programs because such programs increase turnover.
   D. Companies should redesign their compensation strategies to foster career development.

95. Realistic job preview strategies can enhance employee career development and help decrease turnover by:

   A. Informing prospective employees of the organization's compensation and benefits packages.
   B. Helping prospective employees decide whether the job is a good fit with their personal skills and goals.

    C. Explaining the organization's mission, vision, and strategic plans.

    D. Explaining the benefits of the organization's training programs.

96.   HR professionals can most effectively identify employee training needs by conducting:

    A. Both task performance and performance analysis.

    B. Task analysis only.

    C. Performance analysis only.

    D. Neither task analysis nor performance analysis; HR professionals should rely primarily on supervisory recommendations.

97.   HR management practices designed to change employee attitudes, values, and beliefs so that employees can improve the organization are collectively known as:

    A. Organizational development interventions.

    B. Employee training programs.

    C. Organizational reward systems.

    D. Management by objectives.

98.   The performance appraisal method that places employees into predetermined percentages of performance categories is:

    A. Graphic rating scales.

    B. Alternation ranking.

    C. Forced distribution.

    D. Critical incident methods.

99.   Which of the following performance appraisal methods is based on the supervisor's log of positive and negative employee behaviors:

    A. Alternation ranking.

    B. Forced distribution.

    C. Critical incidents.

    D. Behaviorally anchored ranking scales.

100.   A technique to improve deficiencies in employee performance by show-
       ing the employee how to improve when improvement is expected, and
       how results will be evaluated is:

       A. performance action plan.
       B. A demotion confrontation.
       C. Progressive discipline.
       D. Interpersonal sensitivity training.

101.   Organizational pre-retirement counseling programs generally include all
       the following EXCEPT:

       A. Explanation of Social Security benefits.
       B. Financial and investment training.
       C. Counseling in leisure activities.
       D. Psychological testing.

102.   Measurement of the effectiveness of an organization's outplacement
       counseling program would likely include:

       A. Employee performance appraisal records prior to the outplacement
          counseling.
       B. The numbers or percentages of employees placed in new jobs.
       C. The number of employees who were provided with outplacement
          counseling.
       D. The size of the organizational workforce that did not receive outplace-
          ment counseling.

103.   Current trends in the training and development of international employ-
       ees include all the following except:

       A. Increased use of technology in training and development.
       B. Continuing training during the duration of the international assignment.
       C. Increased compensation for international employees.
       D. Increased focus on cultural awareness programs.

104. International employees would be more likely than employees working in the U. S. to receive which of the following training programs:

    A. Safety and security training.
    B. Leadership development programs.
    C. Training in quantitative methodologies.
    D. Training in organizational intranets.

105. The most significant measure of the effectiveness of an employee training program involves:

    A. Determining if employees liked the program
    B. Determining if supervisors liked the program.
    C. Determining if performance improvement was a result of the training or some other factor.
    D. Determining the training costs per employee in attendance.

106. A major consideration in implementing employee performance management and appraisal programs is:

    A. Legal defensibility.
    B. The number of employees who will be appraised.
    C. The size of the company's HR department.
    D. The number of supervisors who will do the appraising.

107. The regulation that makes it unlawful for employers to discriminate against any individual because of race with respect to compensation or other terms of employment is the:

    A. Fair Labor Standards Act.
    B. The 1964 Civil Rights Act.
    C. The Davis-Bacon Act.
    D. The Equal Pay Act.

108. The law created to protect employees against the failure of their employer's pension plan is:

    A. The Equal Pay Act.
    B. ERISA
    C. COBRA.
    D. The Civil Rights Act of 1964

109. A basic principle of organizational compensation practices is that compensation should:

    A. Support organizational strategy by rewarding behaviors the organization values.
    B. Be kept lower than industry standards to increase cost savings.
    C. Focus primarily on seniority.
    D. Be kept separate from union contract issues.

110. If an organization's pay rates are similar to prevailing rates in other organizations, the compensation structure reflects:

    A. Internal equity.
    B. External equity.
    C. Face validity.
    D. Concurrent reliability

111. In conducting a salary survey, HR professionals would likely use all the following EXCEPT:

    A. Formal written surveys.
    B. Telephone surveys.
    C. Commercial salary surveys.
    D. Interviews with former employees.

112. A systematic comparison done to determine the worth of one job relative to another in the organization is:

    A. Job analysis.

B. Job evaluation.

C. A salary survey.

D. Job classification.

113. The simplest method of performing job evaluation is:

A. Ranking.

B. Factor comparison.

C. The point method.

D. A histogram.

114. If organizational exit interviews show that employee turnover is because of dissatisfaction with compensation, HR professionals would likely:

A. Increase pay rates immediately.

B. Conduct a salary survey.

C. Conduct management leadership training.

D. Outsource the compensation and benefits function.

115. A collection of jobs grouped together by approximately equal difficulty levels is a:

A. Pay grade.

B. Pay-for-performance system.

C. Compensation analysis factor.

D. Responsibility level

116. A wage rate that is above the rate range for its grade is known as:

A. A "red circle" job.

B. A "green circle" job.

C. Inadequate compensation.

D. Wage compression.

117. Which of the following is an example of an executive compensation strategy that aims to increase the price of the company's stock:

    A. An increase in base pay.
    B. A company car.
    C. Stock options.
    D. Stock bonuses.

118. A major difference between skill-based pay and pay based on job evaluation is that:

    A. Skill-based pay does not consider seniority.
    B. There are fewer opportunities for advancement with skill-based pay.
    C. Skill-based pay is based on the pay grade for the job.
    D. Skill-based pay is lower than pay based on job evaluation.

119. Broadbanding, as a compensation strategy, is valuable for all the following reasons EXCEPT:

    A. It offers increased flexibility in compensation.
    B. It supports the "boundaryless organization" concept.
    C. It reduces compensation costs.
    D. It supports a flatter organizational hierarchy.

120. An incentive pay plan for factory assembly workers would be most likely to use which of the following methods?

    A. Piecework.
    B. Stock options.
    C. Commission.
    D. Perquisites.

121. Which of the following administrative positions would be considered an "exempt" position under the FLSA?

    A. Entry-level bookkeeper.
    B. Word processor.

C. Office manager.

D. Clerk.

122. A variable pay plan in which a corporation annually contributes shares of stock, which are then distributed to employees when they retire or leave the company, is known as a(n):

A. Profit-sharing plan.

B. Employee stock ownership plan.

C. Individual stock option plan.

D. Flexible benefits plan.

123. All the following are essential to the implementation of an effective incentive plan EXCEPT:

A. Units of work output must be easily measured.

B. Employees must be able to exert control over the work output.

C. Employees must determine the amount of the incentive per unit of work output.

D. Employees must perceive a clear relationship between effort and reward.

124. A disadvantage of incentive plans such as profit-sharing, gain-sharing, and Scanlon plans is that:

A. The link between individual effort and organizational reward is not always clear.

B. Such plans minimize employee commitment to the organization.

C. The plans only benefit executive management.

D. Most employees are not eligible to participate until they are ready to retire.

125. A major compensation consideration for expatriate workers that is NOT generally a consideration for U.S.-based employees is:

A. Wage compression.

B. Geographical pay differentials based on the cost of living.

C. Decreased compensation costs for international employees.

D. The use of incentive plans.

126. A "paid time off" policy that gives each employee a total figure for annual time off, including vacation, sick leave, and personal days to be used at the employee's discretion, will probably result in:

    A. Sharply increased compensation costs.
    B. Increased need for temporary and part-time employees.
    C. Increased costs to administer the policy.
    D. Decreased unscheduled absences.

127. A benefit intended to augment unemployment insurance so that the employee may maintain their standard of living is called:

    A. A Scanlon plan.
    B. Supplemental unemployment benefits.
    C. Workers' compensation.
    D. A cost-of-living allowance.

128. The Family and Medical Leave Act (FMLA) stipulates that:

    A. Workers in organizations of 250 or more employees are eligible for the leave.
    B. Employees may take up to four weeks' leave in a 12-month period.
    C. The leave may be for employee illness or the illness of an employee's spouse or child, but not an employee's parent.
    D. The leave need not be paid by the employer.

129. Methods of reducing workers' compensation costs would include all the following EXCEPT:

    A. Eliminate accident-causing conditions in the workplace.
    B. Get employees back on the job as quickly as possible after an injury or illness.
    C. Discipline employees who file claims for workers' compensation.
    D. Conduct employee safety programs.

130. Regarding employee health care benefits for workers over age 65:

    A. Employers do not have to provide benefits to workers over age 65 because such workers are eligible for Medicare.
    B. Employers must provide the same health care benefits to workers over 65 as they provide to younger workers.
    C. Workers over age 65 are not eligible for employer health care benefits.
    D. Employers may include workers over age 65 in the company's health plan, but the older workers must pay the entire cost of the benefit.

131. Employees who leave an organization are generally eligible to continue their employee health care, at their own expense, for a period of up to 18 months under the provisions of:

    A. COBRA.
    B. ERISA.
    C. FMLA.
    D. FLSA.

132. As the workforce ages, more employees will probably need which of the following benefits?

    A. Child care services.
    B. Long-term care benefits.
    C. Mental health benefits.
    D. Employer-sponsored cafeterias.

133. Employers generally favor defined contribution pension plans over defined benefit pension plans because:

    A. They are easier to administer.
    B. They offer retirees a guaranteed fixed sum at retirement.
    C. The employees' retirement income benefits are predetermined by the employer.
    D. Defined benefit plans include costs for health insurance benefits.

134. An employee benefit that provides employees with counseling and/or treatment for problems such as stress or alcoholism is:

    A. An employee wellness program.
    B. An employee assistance program.
    C. A Scanlon plan.
    D. A defined benefit program.

135. A perquisite that guarantees an executive's salary if the executive's position is eliminated in the event of a merger or acquisition is known as:

    A. Golden parachute.
    B. Golden handcuffs.
    C. A silver chain.
    D. A platinum purse.

136. Flexible benefits plans are also known as:

    A. Employee assistance plans.
    B. Cafeteria plans.
    C. Defined benefits plans.
    D. Health care spending accounts.

137. Regarding employee leasing arrangements, all the following apply EXCEPT:

    A. Benefits costs are much higher with a leasing arrangement.
    B. The leasing firm is the legal employer of the leased workers.
    C. The leasing firm handles employment-related activities, such as recruiting and hiring.
    D. HR administrative costs are reduced in a leasing arrangement.

138. The most commonly used approach to formulating an expatriate worker's pay is to equalize the employee's purchasing power across countries. This is known as:

    A. A cost-benefit analysis.

    B. The balance sheet approach.

    C. International profit-and-loss statements.

    D. Pay equity.

139. Major considerations in the evaluation of expatriate workers' compensation plans generally include all the following EXCEPT:

    A. Evaluating the influence of the costs of living in other countries.

    B. Evaluating the financial incentives needed to attract and keep expatriate workers.

    C. Evaluating the need for repatriation procedures.

    D. Evaluating non-cash compensation items.

140. Lump-sum payments made to reward international employees for moving from one assignment to another are known as:

    A. Hardship allowances.

    B. Foreign service premiums.

    C. Mobility premiums.

    D. Cost-of-living allowances.

141. Groups of health care providers that contract with employers, insurance companies, or third-party payers to deliver health care at a reduced cost are known as:

    A. Health maintenance organizations.

    B. Preferred provider organizations.

    C. Fee-for-service providers.

    D. Health care surrogates.

142. Appropriate steps employers can take to reduce employee health care costs include all the following EXCEPT:

    A. Increase annual health insurance deductibles.

    B. Increase employee contributions to health care costs.

    C. Offer training programs in health and wellness.

    D. Terminate employees who experience significant illness or injury.

143. A salary plus incentive/commission compensation plan would be most appropriate for which of the following workers?

    A. A restaurant chef.
    B. An automobile salesperson.
    C. A registered nurse.
    D. An administrative assistant.

144. The right to purchase a specific number of company stock shares at a specific period for a specific price is known as a(n):

    A. Stock option.
    B. Mega-option grant.
    C. Optional incentive.
    D. Employee stock ownership plan.

145. A one-time payment made to employees terminated by their organization is known as:

    A. Unemployment insurance.
    B. Severance pay.
    C. A commission.
    D. Employee assistance.

146. Employee benefits as a percentage of payroll are currently approximately:

    A. 10% of payroll.
    B. 25% of payroll
    C. 40% of payroll.
    D. 60% of payroll.

147. Unionization tends to be fostered by all the following EXCEPT:

    A. Low employee morale.
    B. Employees' fear of job loss.
    C. Employees' lack of trust in management.
    D. Desire to reduce organizational labor costs.

148. A form of union security in which the company may hire non-union workers, but the workers must join the union after a certain period (if they do not, the workers can be fired) is:

 A. A union shop.
 B. A closed shop.
 C. An open shop.
 D. An agency shop.

149. A union organizing activity in which workers who are employed full time by a union as workplace organizers are hired by unwitting employers is called:

 A. An open shop.
 B. Handbilling.
 C. Union salting.
 D. An unfair labor practice.

150. In union organizing, the group of employees the union will represent is:

 A. The bargaining unit.
 B. The agency shop.
 C. The representation committee.
 D. The solidarity unit.

151. During union organizing activity, the following would be considered an unfair labor practice on the part of a private employer:

 A. Barring union organizers from soliciting employees during their work time.
 B. Barring union organizers from soliciting employees in a public parking lot across the street from the company property.
 C. Barring employees from soliciting other employees during work time.
 D. Barring union organizers from entering the company's executive offices.

152. The federal agency responsible for handling complaints of unfair labor practices in a union environment is:

    A. The National Labor Relations Board.
    B. The Office of Federal Contract Compliance.
    C. The Taft-Hartley Board.
    D. The National Institute for Occupational Safety and Health.

153. An employee dismissal that does not comply with the law or that does not comply with a stated or implied contractual agreement between the company and the employee is called:

    A. Employment-at-will.
    B. Wrongful discharge.
    C. Negligent firing.
    D. Defamation

154. The federal law that governs plant closings in terms of worker layoffs and dismissals is:

    A. The Worker Adjustment and Retraining Notification Act.
    B. The Wagner Act.
    C. The Landrum-Griffin Act.
    D. The Walsh-Healey Act.

155. When companies resort to "bumping" and layoff procedures during a business slowdown, the determination as to which employees should be laid off is usually based on:

    A. Seniority.
    B. Committee consensus.
    C. Managerial discretion.
    D. Employee participatory decision-making.

156. Right-to-work provisions:

    A. Apply to all states in the U.S.

    B. Outlaw provisions that make union membership a condition of keeping one's job.

    C. Are examples of unfair labor practices.

    D. Are prohibited by the Taft-Hartley Act.

157. The president of the U.S. has the right to intervene in:

    A. National emergency strikes.

    B. Wildcat strikes in manufacturing and tourism-related industries.

    C. Economic strikes.

    D. The president may not intervene in any strikes.

158. Common reasons for the failure of an international employee assignment include all the following EXCEPT:

    A. Family's inability to adjust to the international assignment.

    B. Employee's inability to adjust to the international assignment.

    C. Inability to adapt to the local culture.

    D. Dissatisfaction with the performance appraisal process.

159. In dealing with expatriate employees, HR professionals should note that:

    A. Labor relations practices differ from country to country.

    B. Strikes occur much more often in European countries than they do in the U.S.

    C. Grievances occur much more often in European countries than they do in the U.S.

    D. Unions are very rarely found in western Europe.

160. A common repatriation problem for international companies is that:

    A. Repatriation usually precipitates employee grievances.

    B. There is usually high employee turnover following repatriation.

    C. Repatriated employees usually demand significantly higher salaries.

    D. Repatriated employees generally do not wish to return to the U.S.

161. An employee's identification with the company and agreement to pursue the company's mission is termed:

    A. Employee satisfaction.
    B. Employment-at-will.
    C. Employee commitment.
    D. Employee assistance.

162. The current organizational focus on teamwork and employee empowerment should foster behaviors that are necessarily required or rewarded by the organization, but contribute to organizational functioning. These behaviors are known collectively as:

    A. Organizational citizenship.
    B. Total Quality Management.
    C. Grievance prevention actions.
    D. Supervisory enhancements.

163. HR efforts to create positive employee relations can be hindered by:

    A. Negative managerial and supervisory philosophies.
    B. Federal and state workplace laws.
    C. The size of the company.
    D. Location of the company.

164. Activities to encourage employee organizational commitment include all the following EXCEPT:

    A. Promote fair treatment.
    B. Establish the value that people are important in the organization.
    C. Encourage employees to develop to their full potential.
    D. Abolish union activity.

165. Charges of unfair labor practices are filed with the:

    A. Federal district court in the location in which the company is headquartered.

B. National Labor Relations Board.

C. Local police.

D. Union's legal representation team.

166. If an employee files an unfair labor practice charge against a company:

A. The company can file a grievance against the employee.

B. The company may not discriminate against the employee simply because of the filing.

C. Employers may decertify the union.

D. The employee can be demoted, but not fired.

167. Which of the following is FALSE regarding unions?

A. In an open shop, union members do not have to pay union dues.

B. Closed shops are generally illegal except in a few industries.

C. Weekly earnings of union members are usually higher than those of non-union members.

D. Union workers generally enjoy better benefits packages than non-union workers.

168. Collective bargaining requires that union and management negotiate in all the following areas EXCEPT:

A. Wages.

B. Hours of work.

C. Conditions of employment.

D. Stock options offered to management.

169. The most time-consuming strategy in re-negotiating a union contract is usually:

A. The preparation phase prior to the negotiation.

B. The examination of the current labor contract.

C. The negotiation meeting.

D. Communication of the results of the negotiation to employees.

170. all the following are illegal collective bargaining items EXCEPT:

    A. Establishment of a closed shop.
    B. Dismissal of employees based on race.
    C. Discriminatory treatment.
    D. Settlement of unfair labor charges.

171. A court order compelling a party or parties either to resume or desist from a certain action is a(n):

    A. Injunction.
    B. Mandate.
    C. Part of the appeals process.
    D. Result of collective bargaining.

172. A "decision-making leave" may be offered to employees as part of:

    A. The Family and Medical Leave Act.
    B. The union negotiating process.
    C. An employee benefits package.
    D. The employee discipline process.

173. An employee discipline process that emphasizes harsher penalties for repeated infractions is called:

    A. Progressive discipline.
    B. Employment-at-will.
    C. Dismissal and termination.
    D. Escalation of force.

174. With regard to employee communications privacy, HR professionals should note that:

    A. Management monitoring of employee Internet usage is illegal.
    B. Management may not prohibit emergency phone calls from family members.

  C. Employers may be held liable for illegal acts committed by their employees via email.

  D. Continuous videotaping of employees in an office setting is not illegal.

175. Of the following grounds for dismissal, which would likely be most difficult to prove?

  A. Insubordination.
  B. Stealing.
  C. Chronic absenteeism.
  D. Poor quality work.

Answer Key

Q.	1	2	3	4	5	6	7	8	9	10	11	12	13	14	15	16
A.	A	C	C	D	A	B	A	C	A	D	C	D	C	B	A	A

Q.	17	18	19	20	21	22	23	24	25	26	27	28	29	30	31	32
A.	D	A	B	C	B	A	A	B	A	B	A	B	D	A	C	B

Q.	33	34	35	36	37	38	39	40	41	42	43	44	45	46	47	48
A.	B	C	A	C	C	A	D	C	B	B	B	B	A	B	C	A

Q.	49	50	51	52	53	54	55	56	57	58	59	60	61	62	63	64
A.	B	A	B	B	A	A	B	B	C	D	D	A	C	A	D	B

Q.	65	66	67	68	69	70	71	72	73	74	75	76	77	78	79	80
A.	C	B	B	D	A	C	B	D	D	D	A	A	B	A	B	D

Q.	81	82	83	84	85	86	87	88	89	90	91	92	93	94	95	96
A.	C	A	D	B	A	C	B	B	A	A	B	A	A	B	B	A

Q.	97	98	99	100	101	102	103	104	105	106	107	108	109	110	111	112
A.	A	C	C	A	D	B	A	A	C	A	B	B	A	B	D	B

Q.	113	114	115	116	117	118	119	120	121	122	123	124	125	126	127	128
A.	A	B	A	A	C	A	C	A	C	B	C	A	B	D	B	D

Q.	129	130	131	132	133	134	135	136	137	138	139	140	141	142	143	144
A.	C	B	A	B	A	B	A	B	A	B	C	C	B	D	B	A

Q.	145	146	147	148	149	150	151	152	153	154	155	156	157	158	159	160
A.	B	C	D	A	C	A	B	A	B	A	A	B	A	D	A	B

Q.	161	162	163	164	165	166	167	168	169	170	171	172	173	174	175
A.	C	A	A	D	B	B	A	D	A	D	A	D	A	C	A

Answer Explanations

1. A. Through the incorporation of these HR procedures, companies set themselves apart from their rivals, provide their customers with enriched experiences and keep their employees satisfied.

2. C. While an organization's HR personnel can contribute to the correction options A, B, and D, the development and promotion of a company's goods and services do not fall within the purview of this department

3. C. The Title VII of the 1964 Civil Rights Act expressly forbids employers from discriminating against job applicants on grounds of national origin, race, religion, color, or sex.

4. D. The question of who should give workers their paychecks does not constitute a strategic organizational concern on employee remuneration, precisely as it falls within the normal scope of the duties of the HR department.

5. A. Organizational development represents change within a company, which is geared towards strengthening the existing performance or culture, and which involves the active participation of employees.

6. B. Human resource specialists need to know how organizational strategy and staff training are linked. Otherwise, the company's training programs may be ineffective.

7. A. Team building within an organization improves the relationship between employees which in turn makes them more productive. All other options are incorrect.

8. C. This award was instituted to recognize and honor outstanding performance by American businesses, nonprofits, and institutions of higher learning.

9. A. The presence of a strong leader or manager is not a distinctive feature of a self-directed team.

10.   D. The training programs for ISO 9000 make no specific sanctions for staff who fail to meet ISO 9000 requirements.

11.   C. The better the training, the more effective team members would become.

12.   D. Remodeling staff duties to emphasize multitasking, enhanced work, and generalist labor is a great way to effectively reshape the business processes of any enterprise.

13.   C. Flextime is a modern approach to work that lets workers control their workday by picking their own start and end times.

14.   B. This is the only accurate statement from the options because employees in a compressed work week are able to compress their traditional hours into a shorter time frame.

15.   A. An HR audit is one of the best ways to evaluate the efficacy of a company's human resources procedures.

16.   A. According to the BBC, a sizable portion of employees will quit the company within two years of coming home from an overseas assignment. (Mayberry, 2016)

17.   D. The reinforcement of the idea that all world cultures are the same is not a current HR management problem across the globe.

18.   A. The main job of a line manager is to monitor and improve the performance of their team. The primary job of a staff manager is to help and advise line managers on technical matters. HR personnel perform both tasks.

19.   B. The sphere of Corporate HR Management has undergone several changes in the past few decades because many traditional work practices have been replaced by more technological advancements.

20.   C. More employees today exceed the age of retirement than ever before, mostly because, in the wake of the economic unrest and high costs of living today, they cannot afford to retire.

21.   B. The HR department is indispensable throughout an organization's re-structuring processes.

22.   A. Outsourcing HR duties to third-party experts typically costs a company less. The one-time contractual payment is typically less than salary payments that would be made to an employee over the same time frame.

23.   A. HR portals give staff members a single point of access to the HR data kept by the company.

24.   B. Programs for pre-employment training, such as counseling for prospective employees and training in fundamental skills, are crucial aspects of welfare initiatives in a company.

25.   A. Affirmative action is a set of rules meant to stop illegal discrimination against applicants, fix the problems caused by discrimination in the past, and stop discrimination from happening in the future.

26.   B. Substituting a younger worker for an older staff counts as discrimination on the basis of age and is prohibited by the Age Discrimination in Employment Act.

27.   A. The Title VII of the Civil Rights Act of 1964 forbids discrimination in the workplace on grounds of race, color, religion, sex, or national origin.

28.   B. A major clause from the 1991 Civil Rights Act is the introduction of punitive and compensatory damages and the shift of the burden of proof onto employers.

29.   D. The Americans with Disabilities Act forbids any discrimination against anyone who, with or without accommodation, can carry out a job's essential duties.

30.   A. To conduct a successful job analysis, one must first decide how the company will use the data gathered.

31.   C. A job description is a written description of a job's obligations and

responsibilities, including key details like working conditions, safety, and risks. Other options are incorrect.

32. B. The crafting of a job specification and description is the last phase of a successful job analysis.

33. 33. B. Statistical analysis is better than managerial judgment in this regard because it doesn't have any biases that would mess up the results of the observation.

34. C. Ratio analysis evaluates the link between specific variables to calculate how an organization performs over time.

35. A. Major corporations use a hiring yield pyramid to make sure they have a large enough pool of potential employees from which to choose.

36. C. Advertisement in national journals and newspapers is not an effective method of recruiting internal job candidates because it is directed towards external applicants.

37. C. A contingent worker is an individual who is employed on a temporary or fixed-term basis to do certain tasks for a certain project or amount of time. For instance, a freelancer.

38. A. To be valid, a test must effectively perform the task it was intended to perform.

39. D. Under the set of Equal Opportunities laws, employers must demonstrate that there is a clear connection between the tests an applicant must pass to be employed and the role they seek to fill.

40. C. A sample working test is typically used by employers in the direct assessment of an employee's job performance

41. B. Under immigration laws, in order to verify that they are authorized to work in the United States, new hires must complete and submit the I-9 verification forms.

42. B. Unstructured interviews, which are also called "non-directive interviews," don't follow a set pattern, and questions aren't planned ahead of time. The interviewer can ask open-ended questions to collect as much information as possible from the candidates.

43. B. Structured interviews consist of standard, thought-out questions planned ahead of time. As informative as unstructured interviews could be, structured interviews are widely regarded as more valid because they are standardized.

44. B. Being strangers to a job applicant has no effect on the usefulness of a job interview. not knowing the applicant for the position.

45. A is the correct option because succession planning is a strategy for finding and training potential leaders so that they would be able to assume leadership roles in the future when a position opens up.

46. B is the correct option here because according to the labor laws if a company dismisses a worker as a result of his/her default, such a company would not be compelled to pay out benefits to said employee.

47. C is the correct answer because aside from making the new recruits feel at home in the company, the orientation program arms them with the skills to carry out their duties effectively.

48. A. Information about the job descriptions and job specifications are easily shared in this way to ensure that only the candidates who think themselves to be suitable would apply.

49. B is the correct answer because agencies are typically more proactive in their recruitment efforts than internal HR departments are.

50. A is the correct option because flexible working hours blur the divide between work and personal life such that while an employee executes more tasks, it becomes increasingly tougher for them to figure out when the workday ends.

51.   B is the correct answer because a position analysis questionnaire assesses the skills and basic traits that staff members need to have in order to discharge their duties well.

52.   B is the correct option because as stated, the position analysis questionnaire is a standardized strategy used to analyze jobs, quantify employment aspects and correlate them to personality traits.

53.   A. The use of quantitative metrics in job analysis ensures that, even if the tasks are completely different, HR managers can still group them all together and award similar pay to those with similar scores.

54.   A. Relying on a single source of data as an HR professional is bound to produce some inconsistencies.

55.   B. There are far too different classes of unskilled workers, and unlike the skilled workers where certain exam certificates might be part of the standard procedure, there are no such universally acceptable criteria available for unskilled workers.

56.   B. A statistical-based approach gives little room for errors.

57.   C. The definition offered is that of the concept of job rotation.

58.   D. In the scenario raised by the question, options 1-C are more likely to be used than an occupational preferences assessment, because they relate more to the skills an employee would need to survive in the foreign land.

59.   D. An assessment of the reasons for absenteeism in the company presupposes that the staffing needs have been met already.

60.   A. A replacement chart divides staff members into individuals who are fully prepared for a promotion, those who would be ready for a promotion in the future if they got more training, those who are doing a good job but need to be motivated and improve, and those who are not fit for work and must be replaced.

61.   C. From the list provided, it is the most valid and relevant to the position being employed for.

62.   A. Content validity reflects a fair representation of the job responsibilities.

63.   D. Exit interviews are only conducted at the point of dismissal or termination of an employment contract. Not before.

64.   B. Physical therapy departments at universities are good places to get young medical personnel.

65.   C. The advert contravenes the Equal Employment Laws, especially as an insurance sales role is not specific to any gender.

66.   B. While recruiters may be in charge of filling many vacant positions, headhunters attempt to fill high-level executive positions for their clients. They also typically approach and lure away persons who are already working.

67.   B. Data processing requires far more technical knowledge than the other roles mentioned.

68.   D. The ADEA does not affect employment references.

69.   A. The HR division's primary duty is recruitment.

70.   C. Personality tests are reliable indicators of an applicant's stability, introversion, and motivation.

71.   B. The Minnesota multiphasic inventory, the Wonderlic personal characteristics test, and the thematic apperception tests are popular examples of personality tests.

72.   D. Unlike unstructured interviews, structured interviews give the interviewer little room to probe into topics when they come up.

73.   D. The job of an air traffic controller is thoroughly stressful.

74.   D. A Good orientation program can guarantee everything else but that.

75.   A. In Griggs v. Duke Power Company, the supreme court ruled that the tests used in hiring decisions must be connected to the position reasonably.

76.   A. By definition, expatriates are non-citizens of the states where they are employed.

77.   B. Maximizing the parallels between the training environment and the work environment is a strategy through which HR professionals encourage the transmittance of training.

78.   A. A task analysis explicitly shows the needs of a new employee.

79.   B. A performance analysis is a reliable way to confirm if there is a performance issue with an employee and whether training is the best course of action.

80.   D. Inspecting an employee's compensation records is not a way to identify their training needs. The other options are.

81.   C. The sentence identifies the deficiency of a necessary work skill that directly affects the employee's KPI.

82.   A. If an employee cannot execute a task, it is usually because they lack the knowledge, experience, or capacity to follow your direction, and this can be remedied through guidance and training. However, employees who will not perform their duties have issues with commitment or attitude.

83.   D. The compensation received in exchange for doing the work has no place in a performance task analysis.

84.   B. Getting the learner ready for the session is a great way to connect with them and get them to open up before the training starts.

85.   A. Programmed training represents the presentation of information

presented, response collection, and then the provision of feedback on the response.

86. C. Programmed training is typically well-planned and this saves time.

87. B. Expatriates are bound to grapple with cultural differences in the execution of their assignment.

88. B. Even though HR professionals protect and enforce those values, they are not expected to redefine their company's mission and objectives.

89. A. Assessing employee performance before and after a training initiative would show how well the training was received.

90. A. All effective job appraisals must begin with a definition of the job role and responsibilities.

91. B. This kind of assessment includes the qualities needed for the position and asks the user to rank the applicant on each quality, such as reliability and resourcefulness.

92. A as it lists out the best order for assessing performance management.

93. A. Peer performance evaluation and self-appraisal are effective ways to encourage employee participation.

94. B. Contemporary HR development initiatives serve not just the needs of the organization, but also help employees plot their professional growth.

95. B. Conducting realistic job previews can help applicants decide the roles best suited to their personal abilities and goals.

96. A. An analysis of task performance and performance analysis is a reliable way to identify the training needs of staff members.

97. A. Organizational development measures are a fundamentally

holistic process that enables corporations to improve their adaptability and performance.

98. C. Forced distribution is the approach to performance evaluation that assigns staff to specified percentages of performance areas.

99. C. Critical incidents, by definition, is a performance evaluation strategy that relies on the supervisor's log of both good and bad employee behaviors.

100. A. A performance action plan as a technique increases the performance of employees by demonstrating how to improve when progress is expected and how it will be assessed.

101. D. Out of all options provided, psychological testing is not a part of organizational pre-retirement counseling programs.

102. B. The volume of workers assigned to new jobs is a direct representation of the success or failure of a company's outplacement counseling program.

103. A. The use of technology in training is not a trend in worldwide employee training or development.

104. A. In several respects, security and safety training is more relevant to expatriates than their U.S.-based colleagues.

105. C. It is the most important indicator of a training program's effectiveness.

106. A. This consideration will help HR personnel reduce the susceptibility of their company to legal issues.

107. B. The Civil Rights Act of 1964 prohibits employers from treating any individual unfairly due to race regarding pay or other conditions of work.

108. B. The ERISA was enacted to safeguard employees from the insolvency of their employers' pension schemes.

109.   A. The goal of a sound compensation policy is to support an organizational strategy by recognizing and rewarding desirable actions.

110.   B. When workers in a company receive equitable compensation compared to others who carry out comparable tasks in other companies, external equity is deemed attained.

111.   D. Ex-employees have no active role to play in salary polls.

112.   B. A job evaluation is a methodical comparison used to establish the relative value of one job vs another inside a company.

113.   A. With ranking, jobs are evaluated based on how valuable they are to the company.

114.   B. The results of a salary survey in this case will shed more light on the stance of current employees on the issue.

115.   A. A company's pay grades are a collection of positions that are paid at the same or a similar rate and possess roughly the same relative internal value.

116.   A. A red circle job attracts a wage rate higher than the range for its grade.

117.   C. Employee stock options (ESOs) allow workers to purchase a predetermined amount of shares of a corporation's stock at a predetermined price, and are aimed at raising the value of all company stock.

118.   A. Seniority is typically not considered if the remuneration strategy is based on skills.

119.   C. Broadbanding salary structures have a broader salary range between the lowest and highest salary tiers, but there are fewer salary tiers overall.

120.   A. Piecework is a job type where employees are compensated based on how many items they produce or how many jobs they finish. Put differently, workers receive payment piece-by-piece.

121. C. An office manager falls under the FLSA's definition of an "exempt" position in Section 13 (a) (1).

122. B. Employee stock ownership plans (ESOPs) provide employees with company equity, frequently based on how long they have worked for the organization. Shares typically vest at a specific time after the employment contract.

123. C. Though desirable, employee input is not a condition for the success of an incentive plan.

124. A is a major disadvantage of Scanlon incentive plans.

125. B. Geographical salary disparity arising from the cost of living in foreign countries is a major consideration in deciding the compensation for expatriates.

126. D. A reduction in unscheduled absences is a possible outcome of a paid time off policy.

127. B. Supplemental unemployment benefits are meant to supplement unemployment insurance and allow an employee to retain their level of living.

128. D. Under the FMLA, an employer is not obligated to pay for an employee's leave.

129. C. Disciplining staff members who file workers' compensation claims cannot be used to lower workers' compensation costs,

130. B. Under the ADEA, employers are required to offer such older employees the same benefits as they do younger employees.

131. A. COBRA safeguards the employee health insurance of people who resign from their roles for a maximum of 18 months

132. B as it will be needed by employees as they age.

133. A. Defined contribution pension plans are easier to manage than defined benefits pension plans.

134. B. Employees' assistance programs make counseling and/or therapy opportunities available to employees with issues like stress and alcoholism.

135. A. Golden parachutes are a form of remuneration offered to key executives when a public company is sold and they resign or have their duties significantly reduced.

136. B. Flexible benefits plans are also called cafeteria plans.

137. A. Although leases require additional interest payments, they are not always less pricey than making a sizable lump sum payment up ahead.

138. B. The balance sheet method is a way to determine an expatriate worker's compensation by equalizing the worker's purchasing power across nations

139. C. Determining whether repatriation procedures are necessary is not considered in evaluating the expatriate workers' compensation scheme

140. C. Mobility premiums are payments made to international workers as incentives for switching assignments.

141. B. Preferred provider organizations are specific healthcare plans that enter into agreements with medical service providers, like medical centers, to build a network of participating providers. Using providers in the network of the insurance plan lowers your costs.

142. D. The termination of sick workers to lower healthcare expenses is unlawful and could lead to litigations.

143. B. A salesperson for automobiles can earn a consistent, defined annual salary that they can supplement with a percentage from their sales.

144. A. A stock option represents a person's right to buy a specific number of stock shares at a certain price and time.

145. B. Severance pay is a one-time payment made to employees who have been let go by their employer.

146. C is the current ratio of employee benefits to payroll.

147. D as it does not encourage unionization.

148. A. The definition presented represents a union shop.

149. C. Union salting is a union activity in which employers unknowingly recruit full-time union activists.

150. A. A bargaining unit is a collection of employees with distinct and recognizable shared interests, represented by one labor union in interactions with the management.

151. B. It is an unfair labor practice by a private employer during union-organizing activities.

152. A. The National Labor Relations Board is the federal institution in charge of addressing grievances regarding unfair labor practices in a union setting.

153. B. Such a termination qualifies as a wrongful discharge.

154. A. The WARN Act is the federal statute regulating plant closures in terms of employee dismissals and layoffs.

155. A. Businesses use "bumping" when they go through a restructuring to keep their top performers by allowing those with more seniority to apply for roles otherwise occupied by others with less senior staff.

156. B. Right-to-work regulations typically prohibit clauses that make union membership a condition for retaining employment.

157. A. The US president has the constitutional powers to interfere in national emergency strikes.

158. D is not a reason for the failure of expatriate assignments.

159. A. Of all the options, it is the most relevant for HR interaction with expatriate workers.

160. B is a serious challenge for multinational corporations.

161. C. An employee's commitment refers to how well they identify with and commit to the organization's mission.

162. A as it represents an employee's voluntary engagement with a company or organization that is separate from their contractual obligations.

163. A. It has no bearing on HR attempts to foster good employee relations.

164. D. Banning union activity does not promote organizational commitment among employees

165. B. The National Labor Relations Board is the agency tasked with regulating labor practices.

166. B. It is prohibited by labor laws.

167. A. Union members still pay dues in an open shop. All other statements are correct.

168. D. Stock options that were offered to the management fall outside the scope of collective bargaining with unions.

169. A is the most time-consuming method for the renegotiation of a union contract.

170. D is negotiable with collective bargaining.

171. A. An injunction is a legal and just relief that forces parties to perform or refrain from performing particular activities.

172. D is closely linked to the decision-making leave.

173. A. Progressive discipline emphasizes tougher punishments for recurrent violations.

174. C. Under labor laws, employers can be held accountable for criminal conduct committed over email by their workers.

175. A. It is very challenging to recognize insubordination at work because it occurs in different forms.

Chapter Eight: Full-Length Practice Test #2

Instructions

These questions below have been included to prepare you for the PHR exam, and test your knowledge of the major test areas we've already discussed in the preceding chapters of this book. Check the answers for this practice test in the answer key section (below the test) to get immediate feedback. There are 175 questions in all, the first 25 questions are pretest questions and your answers to them would not count towards the determination of your final test score.

Total exam time: three hours.

1. During the organization of a union, it's possible that the union will gain recognition from the management. The management is then obliged to give the NLRB a list of employees who are eligible to vote in the unionization election. What is the name of the list of such employees called?

    A. Constituent List.
    B. Union prospectus List.
    C. Excelsior List.
    D. Candidate List

2.   There are four components of the HR Impact Model, which affect how an HR Professional may operate within a given environment. Which one of the following is NOT a component of the HR Impact Model?

   A. Consultation.
   B. Client.
   C. Catalyst.
   D. Programs and processes

3.   Holly is a senior worker in her organization and she is a member of the union. Her position will be eliminated in sixty days and she will be released from the company. Rather than being unemployed, Holly asks the union to move her to a less senior position and release a junior employee. If the union agrees to this, what will this term be known as?

   A. Bumping.
   B. Displacement.
   C. Releasing.
   D. Re-organization

4.   As an HR Professional, you must be familiar with the collective bargaining agreements and the process that rights are given, contracts, and union and management cooperation. Consider an arbitration process between the management and the union. What term is assigned to resolving the disagreement by an arbitrator's interpretation of the language of the contract?

   A. Resolution.
   B. Interpretation.
   C. Decision.
   D. Outcome

5. As an HR Professional, you must be familiar with several lawsuits and their effect on human resource practices today. What legal case found that a test that has an adverse impact on a protected class is still lawful as long as the test can be valid and job-related?

    A. Washington versus Davis, 1976.
    B. Griggs versus Duke Power, 1971.
    C. McDonnell Douglas Corp. versus Green, 1973.
    D. Albemarle Paper versus Moody, 1975.

6. Your organization has a retirement benefits plan covered by ERISA. Under ERISA, which of the following is your organization required to do for the plan participants?

    A. Provide each participant with plan information, specifically about the features and funding of the plan through a summary plan description at the cost of only $7 per participant, per year.
    B. Provide each participant with plan information, specifically about the features and funding of the plan through a summary plan description at no cost.
    C. Provide each participant with monthly plan information, specifically about the features and funding of the plan through a summary plan description of only $7 per participant, per month.
    D. Provide each participant with monthly plan information, specifically about the features and funding of the plan through a summary plan description at no cost.

7. Fran is an HR Professional for her organization and she is interviewing applicants for a warehouse position. One candidate has written on his application that he speaks Spanish. Fran interviews this candidate in Spanish and interviews all other candidates in English. This is an example of what?

    A. Disparate treatment.
    B. Disparate impact.
    C. Accommodation.
    D. Perpetuating past discrimination

8. As a Senior HR Professional, you should be familiar with the non-monetary rewards that your company provides for its employees. Which of the following is an example of a non-monetary reward?

    A. Satisfaction with challenging and exciting assignments.
    B. Esteem from working with other talented people.
    C. Cash compensation.
    D. On-site cafeteria

9. Your organization will be using the point factor technique in its evaluations of job performance. You need to communicate what the point factor technique accomplishes as you're the HR Professional for your organization. Which one of the following best describes the point factor technique?

    A. Specific compensable factors are identified and then performance levels within the factors are documented.
    B. Specific compensable factors are identified and then performance levels within the factors are weighted on the importance to the employee.
    C. Performance factors are identified by the employee and then performance levels within the factors are weighted based on importance to the organization.
    D. Specific compensable factors are identified and then performance levels within the factors are documented. The different factors and levels are weighted based on importance to the organization.

10. What is the Fair Pay amount that defines what a person makes, to be considered highly compensated?

    A. $110,000 or more.
    B. $150,000 or more.
    C. $100,000 or more.
    D. $125,000 or more.

11.   A more positive workplace can be created if managers and supervisors communicate to employees exactly what their jobs require in terms of performance. This kind of communication is called:

A. Employee engagement.
B. Expectation clarity.
C. The discipline process.
D. An exit survey.

12.   A commonly used method of measuring employees' perceptions of fair treatment is:

A. An employee opinion survey.
B. An examination of employee dismissal records.
C. Examining utilization records of employee assistance programs.
D. Examining absenteeism rates.

13.   A major indicator of management commitment to fair treatment in the workplace is:

A. The degree to which employees feel they can take part in decisions that affect them.
B. Frequency of employee social activities in the workplace.
C. The size of the workforce.
D. The frequency of performance appraisal.

14.   Prior to beginning an employee discipline process, HR professionals should encourage managers to:

A. Give the employee a written warning.
B. Make sure the evidence supports the charge of wrongdoing.
C. Give the employee a verbal warning.
D. Conduct a formal employee performance appraisal.

15.   A conflict resolution technique in which a neutral third party attempts to assist the conflicting parties in reaching an agreement is:

A. Mediation
B. Cooperation.
C. Arbitration.
D. Dissolution

16.   The conflict resolution technique, which guarantees a solution to an impasse by dictating the terms of the settlement, is:

A. Mediation.
B. Arbitration.
C. Conciliation.
D. Grievance resolution.

17.   An example of management's failure to bargain in good faith with a union is:

A. Bypassing the union representative.
B. Refusing to allow a closed shop.
C. Demanding that the two parties discuss severance pay.
D. Proposing drug testing of employees.

18.   The union decertification process is:

A. Essentially similar to the union certification process.
B. Similar to the union certification process, except that a higher percentage of votes is needed to decertify the union that was needed to certify the union.
C. A complex procedure that usually results in failure.
D. Currently illegal under the Wagner Act.

19.   An appropriate action for employers attempting to avoid unionization would be to:

A. Threaten employees with the loss of their jobs if they unionize.

B. Provide supervisory training regarding unfair labor practices and management effectiveness /leadership training.

C. Decrease compensation as a punishment for union organizing activity.

D. Initiate small but strategic layoffs.

20. In general, employees who feel they are treated fairly will:

    A. Be more likely to unionize.
    B. Be less likely to file grievance charges.
    C. Be more productive.
    D. Be absent less often.

21. Research has shown that employees of hostile or abusive supervisors are more likely than other employees to do all the following EXCEPT:

    A. Report high-stress levels.
    B. Quit their jobs.
    C. Report lower satisfaction with life.
    D. Participate in employee training programs.

22. An appropriate technique HR professionals can use to increase employee involvement in workplace improvement initiatives is to:

    A. Foster an atmosphere of open communication and invite employee input.
    B. Create employee discipline guidelines for those who do not participate.
    C. Enlarge the jobs of those who refuse to participate in involvement activities.
    D. Involve only managers and supervisors in workplace improvement initiatives.

23. Managers who need to disseminate specific information quickly throughout the organization should use which of the following communication approaches?

    A. Top-down communication.
    B. Bottom-up communication.
    C. Quality circles.

D. Employee participatory management.

24. An abnormal health condition caused by exposure to environmental factors associated with employment is a(n):

    A. Occupational illness.
    B. Repetitive stress injury.
    C. Health citation.
    D. Malingering

25. The federal law that most specifically and comprehensively addresses workplace health and safety is:

    A. OSHA.
    B. ADA.
    C. COBRA.
    D. ERISA

26. If an employee is injured at work, the most appropriate initial action would be to:

    A. Provide first aid followed by medical attention.
    B. Notify the company's legal defense team.
    C. Notify OSHA.
    D. Consult the employee's benefits package to determine health coverage.

27. Identification of employee alcohol abuse:

    A. Is often difficult, as symptoms such as tardiness can occur with other kinds of behavior problems and alcohol abuse.
    B. Should be done routinely with blood alcohol screenings.
    C. Should be grounds for immediate dismissal.
    D. Should trigger a formal disciplinary proceeding.

28. The federal Drug-Free Workplace Act requires:

    A. Employers with federal contracts or grants to ensure drug-free workplaces.

B. Monthly drug testing for all employees.

C. Immediate dismissal if an employee is determined to have used drugs in the past.

D. Random searches for illegal substances in the workplace.

29.   Positive steps employers can take to reduce workplace violence include all the following EXCEPT:

A. Providing workplace safety and security training.

B. Creating an organizational culture that emphasizes mutual respect.

C. Refusing to hire employees who have ever been arrested for any type of violent act.

D. Providing security staff to monitor the workplace.

30.   If an OSHA inspector shows up at the workplace, one of the first steps an HR professional should take is:

A. To check the inspector's credentials.

B. Notify the company's lawyer.

C. Correct any violation noted by the inspector.

D. Volunteer to provide all health and safety-related company records.

31.   A major concern in occupational respiratory illness is:

A. Colds and flu spread by fellow employees.

B. Workplace asbestos contamination.

C. Workplace silica contamination.

D. AIDS.

32.   An organization that employs many workers who smoke cigarettes should note all the following EXCEPT:

A. Smokers have higher absenteeism rates than nonsmokers.

B. Organizations that have significant numbers of smokers generally pay higher health and fire insurance premiums.

C. Instituting a ban on hiring smokers is generally illegal under federal law.

D. Smokers have greater risks for occupational accidents than nonsmokers.

33. A special health and safety concern for expatriate employees, more so than those in the U.S., is:

    A. Possible security threats in foreign countries.
    B. Chemical exposure.
    C. Cigarette smoking.
    D. Alcohol abuse.

34. HR professionals who work in fast-paced organizations should do all the following EXCEPT:

    A. Monitor employees for signs of stress and burnout.
    B. Provide training programs in burnout prevention.
    C. Try to give employees more control over their jobs.
    D. Report employees who seek help with stress-related problems to their supervisors.

35. Employers who reward employees for increasing the number of days without a workplace injury:

    A. Will probably have a safer workplace.
    B. May not do so without union oversight if the company is unionized.
    C. Are governed by OSHA.
    D. Must communicate reward policies in writing.

36. Your organization has 80 full-time employees. Management has recently informed you they have sold their business and they'll be releasing all employees in the organization. Based on the Worker Adjustment and Retraining Notification Act of 1988, how many days must management give in writing to the employees of this organization before the mass layoff?

    A. 60 days
    B. 120 days
    C. Zero days
    D. 30 days

37. As an HR Professional, you must be familiar with several acts of congress, laws, and regulations that address risks in the workplace. Which of the following laws was the first to establish consistent safety standards for workers?

    A. Mine Safety and Health Act
    B. USA Patriot Act
    C. Occupational Safety and Health Act
    D. Homeland Security Act

38. What nonmathematical forecasting technique uses rounds of anonymous surveys among participants to determine consensus on the direction of employment trends, candidate selection, or other forecasting topics?

    A. Delphi Technique
    B. Qualitative forecast
    C. Management forecast
    D. Trend analysis

39. Which of the following are the benefits of gainsharing programs? Each correct answer represents a complete solution. Choose three.

    A. Aligns employees to organization goals
    B. Employees are paid based on group performance rather than individual performance
    C. Enhances employees' focus and awareness
    D. Helps organization to achieve improvement in key performance measures

40. Jane is preparing for an interview process for an open position within her company. Jane has prepared several questions for the interview. In her questions, Jane is careful not to ask all the following questions, except for which one?

    A. Our hours are from 8 AM to 5 PM. Can you meet this requirement for the position?
    B. Where are you from?
    C. How many children do you have?

D. What's your date of birth?

41. You have just hired a job candidate for a position in your company. You are now required by the Immigration and Control Act of 1986 to complete an employment eligibility form to verify the new employee's eligibility to work in the United States. Within how many days must you complete this form?

    A. 3 days
    B. 30 days
    C. 7 days
    D. 10 days.

42. Holly and Gary are HR Professionals in their organization and they're working to develop the strategic plan for their organization. Holly and Gary are using SWOT analysis to help understand the needs of human, financial, technological, capital, and other aspects of their organization. What is SWOT?

    A. SWOT is an analysis to define the schedule, weaknesses, opportunities, and timetable of a project endeavor.
    B. SWOT is an analysis to define the strengths, weaknesses, opportunities, and threats an organization may face.
    C. SWOT is an analysis to define the strengths, weaknesses, openness, and timeliness of an organization.
    D. SWOT is an analysis to define the seriousness, weaknesses, openness, and timetable of organization development.

43. Validity is an important part of the interview process. All HR Professionals should recognize validity through the interview process. Which one of the following is not one of the four types of validity?

    A. Content validity
    B. Professional validity
    C. Construct validity
    D. Predictive validity

44. You are an HR Professional for your organization. You and your supervisor are reviewing the EEO reporting requirements for your company to comply with the reports your firm should file. Which report is collected on an odd-number of years from state and local governments?

    A. EEO-4 Report
    B. EEO-1 Report
    C. EEO-5 report
    D. EEO-3 Report

45. Sally is an HR Professional for an organization and she's working with Holly, another HR Professional. Holly is concerned with the effectiveness of a new policy. Sally is concerned with the efficiency of the new policy. What is the difference between effectiveness and efficiency?

    A. These are the same values in human resources.
    B. Efficiency is doing things right. Effectiveness is doing the right things.
    C. Efficiency is being effective when doing things. Effectiveness is doing the right things efficiently.
    D. Efficiency is knowing what to do. Effectiveness is doing what you know you should.

46. As an HR Professional, you must recognize and be aware of several pieces of legislation that affect your performance as HR Professional. Which one of the following acts used the terminology 'work now, grieve later' to describe the urgency of performing work?

    A. Clayton Act
    B. National Labor Relations Act
    C. Railway Labor Act
    D. National Industrial Recovery Act

47. The Fair and Accurate Credit Transactions Act (FACT) covers the use of _____ in workplace investigations.

    A. Recording devices.
    B. Video surveillance

C. Third party investigators.

D. Polygraph machines.

48. Which of the following is not part of the TIPS acronym concerning unfair labor practices?

A. promise

B. interrogate

C. threaten

D. slander

49. Union security clauses protect:

A. employers

B. union employees

C. union jobs

D. unions

50. Which act extended collective bargaining rights to federal employees?

A. Clayton Act

B. Labor-Management Relations Act

C. Civil Service Reform Act

D. Landrum-Griffin Act

51. Which of the following is injuring someone's reputation by making a false and malicious statement?

A. Defamation

B. Derogatory utterance

C. Libel

D. Slander

52. A closed shop clause states that union membership is a condition of hiring is:

A. Legal in all cases

B. Illegal (except in the construction industry)

C. Legal (except in the construction industry)

D. Illegal in all cases

53. The principle that employers have the right to hire, fire, demote, and promote whomever they choose for any reason is called:

A. Implied contract

B. Employment-at-will

C. Just cause

D. Common-law

54. The process of sending employees abroad and supporting their ability to
adapt to cultural changes while they complete their assignment is called:

A. Culture shock

B. Expatriation

C. International assignment

D. Internationalization

55. Career planning focuses upon the needs of which of the following groups?

A. HR professionals

B. Managers

C. Employees

D. The company/organization.

56. What term describes the illegal agreement between management and a
potential employee to offer the potential employee a job as long as they
agree not to join a union?

A. Non-union agreement

B. Double-breasted agreement

C. Scab contract

D. Yellow dog contract.

57. A code of ethics will not be effective if

   A. The organization adopts a one-size-fits-all approach.
   B. It omits statements relative to how the code will be implemented and upheld.
   C. The CEO does not write the introduction to and/or cover letter accompanying the code.
   D. It includes components that could be perceived as threatening or punitive.

58. Of the risk management techniques, which is defined as an act of stopping or not attempting a business activity that may or may not result in some kind of loss?

   A. Transferability
   B. Avoidance
   C. Retention
   D. Accepting the consequences of the potential risks.

59. In what kind of transaction is a contract provided by an entity that is not otherwise involved in the agreement?

   A. Request for proposal
   B. Terminal contract
   C. Third-party contract
   D. Bought contract.

60. What is the correct term for the process of identifying risks and taking effective steps to minimize them?

   A. Risk assessment
   B. Risk strategy
   C. Risk management
   D. Liability assessment.

61. Sione earns roughly $22,000 per year, manages and supervises three other employees, and spends about 35 hours per week on job duties that require a fair amount of discretion and independence. Which of the following is true about Sione?

    A. Sione is nonexempt, based on the salary requirements.
    B. Sione is exempt because he manages and supervises other employees.
    C. Sione is exempt, because of his salary.
    D. Sione is nonexempt, because of a lack of hours.

62. Of the following, which is an OSHA standard that provides guidelines for preparing a corporate emergency action plan and creates specifications for unobstructed means of exit from any point in a company's building?

    A. Means of Egress standard
    B. The General Duty Standard.
    C. Specifications for Accident Prevention standard
    D. Hazard Communication standard.

63. What is the correct term for a statistical HR measurement that assesses productivity?

    A. Revenue per employee
    B. Loss per employee
    C. Cost per hire
    D. Ratio of total employees to HR staff.

64. Which of the following acts allows employers to follow drug testing and drug-free workplace policies to ensure a healthy workplace for all?

    A. The Occupational Safety and Health Act
    B. The Drug-Free Workplace Act
    C. Federal Employers Liability Act
    D. Worker Adjustment and Retraining Notification Act.

65. Offshoring refers to:

   A. Outsourcing to third-party providers whose corporate headquarters are located overseas
   B. Another term for outsourcing
   C. Moving part or all the functions of a firm overseas, but maintaining corporate governance of those entities
   D. Outsourcing to firms that primarily conduct business at their own worksite.

66. Blake-Mouton's situational leadership theory

   A. Measures and assesses concern for the needs of direct reports and concern for the accomplishment of tasks.
   B. Identifies "impoverished managers" as ones who have not been given the opportunity to engage in training opportunities designed to enhance essential supervisory skills.
   C. Uses a 10-point scale along each axis.
   D. Builds upon Hersey and Blanchards' model.

67. During the strategic planning process, it is often necessary to use a PEST analysis. What is PEST an acronym for?

   A. Political, economic, social, technology.
   B. Personal, environmental, strategic, technology.
   C. Private, efficiency, strategic, turnover rate
   D. Productivity, efficiency, strategic, task structure.

68. What did the McDonnell-Douglas Corp. v. Green case establish?

   A. Adverse treatment
   B. Disparate treatment
   C. Unfair labor practices
   D. That companies could not discriminate against women based upon childbearing status.

69. Of the following acts, which one requires that companies with federal construction contracts must pay their laborers and mechanics the standard wage of employees in the geographic area in which the work is being performed?

    A. The Fair Labor Standards Act
    B. McNamara-O'Hara Service Act
    C. Federal Labor Relations Act
    D. The Davis-Bacon Act

70. A competitor has recently hired three of your company's employees. An email is sent to all remaining employees reminding them of their obligation to protect proprietary information to which they are exposed when performing their jobs, and that disciplinary action up to and including termination could result from a violation of this policy.

    Shortly thereafter, a fourth employee interviews with a different competitor. The employee knows they could present themself better by discussing current research and development projects on which they are working. The employee decides, however, not to discuss information about these projects with the interviewers. This represents an example of:

    A. Negative reinforcement
    B. Positive reinforcement
    C. Punishment
    D. Extinction.

71. What kind of statement describes what an organization does and how that differs from what other organizations may do?

    A. Mission statement
    B. Corporate strategy
    C. Core competencies
    D. Vision statement.

72. A manager with whom you have not previously worked comes to you for help with implementing two different solutions she has come up with to fix a turnover problem in her department. This manager is highly regarded and highly visible in the organization. You are eager to perform well on this project because you are confident it will help you forge a relationship with this manager. You are also certain that the manager will tell her peers about her experience with you, which makes it particularly critical that you handle yourself well. Your first response should be to:

    A. Communicate your commitment to implementing the manager's solution.
    B. Offer alternative solutions based on the experience you have had in similar situations.
    C. Ask questions to get more information about the problems the manager is experiencing.
    D. Ask questions to get information that will help you implement the manager's solution more effectively.

73. What two terms are generally used interchangeably to describe methods for obtaining any information that may be necessary to make decisions that will best allow the organization to accomplish its goals?

    A. Needs organization and needs assessment
    B. Organizational assessment and organizational analysis
    C. Needs analysis and organizational approach
    D. Needs assessment and needs analysis.

74. Which of the following is the best quality tool for gathering information about a specific problem?

    A. Pareto chart
    B. Ishikawa diagram
    C. A cause-and-effect diagram
    D. Scatter charts.

75. An OSHA violation with a substantial probability of death or serious physical harm as the result of a workplace hazard is which of the following?

    A. Willful
    B. Serious
    C. Repeat
    D. De-minimus.

76. Which of the following does Maslow identify as each person's most fundamental need?

    A. Basic physical needs
    B. Esteem
    C. Recognition
    D. A living wage.

77. If an employee is entitled to minimum wage, protections under child labor and equal pay, and overtime if he or she works over 40 hours per week, is the employee exempt or non-exempt?

    A. Exempt
    B. Non-exempt.

78. Which of the following is not an element of a SMART goal?

    A. Measurable
    B. Specific
    C. Rational
    D. Achievable

79. Which of the following questions must be addressed in a needs analysis to select an HRIS?

    A. Will the system share any data with other systems in the company?
    B. What information will be an input into the HRIS?
    C. Who will have access to the information in the HRIS?
    D. all the above.

80. Sometimes, an employee might choose to no longer have the union represent them. If this is the case, what must the employee petition the NLRB for?

    A. Deauthorization
    B. Decertification
    C. A voluntary recognition bar
    D. A blocking-charge bar

81. You're the HR manager at your organization and report directly to the president (whose sister died of cancer about six months ago). One afternoon, an employee comes to you with a problem. Her sister (who lives out of state) has been diagnosed with a very aggressive form of cancer and has less than 6 months to live.

    The employee wants to spend the last few months of her sister's life with her, to share time and care for her in her final days. The employee has already requested a leave of absence but was advised by an HR representative and her manager that this sort of leave isn't covered under FMLA. Your department is going into its "busy season," so her manager is unwilling to grant any other type of leave.

    She is concerned about how she will support herself while she is staying with her sister. She asks you whether it is possible for the company to call this a layoff and approve of her getting unemployment insurance. Sadly, she knows her sister won't live longer than six months, so unemployment insurance benefits would carry her through. After you express your concern and sympathy, which of the following responses would be the best?

    A. Tell the employee that it is up to the state, not the company, whether unemployment insurance will be granted and that, while you sympathize with her situation on a personal level, it's not possible for you to code the termination as a layoff.
    B. Tell the employee that it's up to the state, not the company, whether unemployment insurance will be granted. However, as long as the president approves (and you're pretty sure he will), you're willing to code the termination as a layoff.

C. As HR, your role is that of employee advocate, and you will advocate on her behalf to the president. You are fairly confident that he will approve this request and will get back to the employee either way as soon as possible.

D. You remind the employee, as gently as possible, that, as HR, your role is to ensure that all the company's policies and procedures are followed, and falsifying the termination code would violate policy. You just can't code the termination as a layoff.

82. Which of the following is the concept that recognized that businesses are social organizations and economic systems and recognized that employee productivity was directly related to job satisfaction?

    A. Human relations
    B. Human resource management
    C. Human resource strategy
    D. Strategic management.

83. You've accepted a position as the HR manager with a small manufacturing organization. You were acquainted with the former HR manager and you're excited to be following in his footsteps at his former company. From everything he has told you, the company had everything in line regarding HR-related issues, including safety issues, EEO reports, I-9 documentation, sound compensation practices, etc. You are surprised when you then come across documentation stating that the organization was cited for a "Serious Violation" three months earlier. You are concerned because you know that a serious violation is:

    A. The most serious category of violation recognized by the Department of Justice.
    B. One that the employer either knew about or should have known about.
    C. Unlikely to result in death, but is likely to result in serious injury.
    D. Considered by the EEOC to be deliberate and intentional.

84. When does a lockout occur?

    A. When the union shuts down the workplace.

B. When the employer refuses to allow the union to unionize the premises

C. When employees refuse to work

D. When the employer shuts down the workplace entrances, keeping employees from working.

85. Which of the following, developed by a behavioral scientist, explains how people meet their various needs through work?

A. The Hierarchy of Work

B. The Meaning of Work

C. The Hierarchy of Needs

D. Needs, Wants, and Work.

86. Which of the following federal laws prohibits featherbedding?

A. The Norris-LaGuardia Act

B. The Taft-Hartley Act

C. Title VII

D. The Wagner Act.

87. How can an employer determine whether a job creates an ergonomic hazard for an employee?

A. Review and analyze the OSHA logs

B. Review and analyze the worker's compensation records

C. Review the MSDS

D. Observe the incumbent performing the job duties.

88. What Act requires all government contractors with contracts exceeding $10,000 (for everything that is not construction work) to pay their employees the real, prevailing wage for their locality, as established by the Secretary of Labor?

A. Service Contract Act

B. Walsh Healey Public Contracts Act

C. Fair Labor Standards Act

D. Davis Bacon Act.

89. When are materials first protected under U.S. copyright law?

    A. When the work is first received by any person other than the producer.
    B. When the work is first saved electronically or printed.
    C. When the work is first registered with the U.S. Copyright office.
    D. When the work is first published.

90. Which motivational theory surmises that people are motivated only by the reward they will receive when they succeed and that they will constantly weigh the value of that reward against the effort they believe is required to achieve it?

    A. The ERG Theory
    B. The Expectancy Theory
    C. The Motivation/Hygiene Theory
    D. The Equity Theory.

91. What is conductive discharge?

    A. The employee is told to resign with positive feedback and a reference
    B. The employee is paid for at least 2 months after discharge
    C. The employee resigns due to poor behavior by their employer
    D. The employee is no longer allowed on the construction site
    E. None of the above.

92. In behavioral leadership theories, the dimension of leadership behavior known as initiating structure or job-related refers to

    A. The interpersonal relationships that managers must first establish with employees before attempting to ensure the completion of the actual work
    B. What employees need to do, and how they need to do it, to attain objectives
    C. The training in which managers need to participate to develop the skills needed to be an effective leader
    D. The degree to which an individual shows an innate ability to be an effective leader.

93. Eliza Doolittle, the HR director at One Enormous Chair, is analyzing various employee reports that identify the staffing needs, training needs, and career progression of the company's current employees. Which forecasting model is Eliza using?

    A. Delphi technique
    B. Lateral thinking
    C. Future map
    D. Scenario analysis.

94. Which type of learning curve initially begins slowly, with smaller learning increments, but generally increases in pace and with larger increments as learning proceeds?

    A. Negatively accelerating learning curve
    B. S-shaped learning curve
    C. Positively accelerating learning curve
    D. Plateau learning curve.

95. Most likely, which of the following employees would take part in vestibule training?

    A. A cashier
    B. A teacher's assistant
    C. A marketing manager
    D. An outside sales representative.

96. A 16-year-old son of one of your friends is looking for a summer job and has been offered a job at your employer, a coal mine. Which of the following makes this job offer illegal?

    A. Mine Safety and Health Act
    B. Occupational Safety and Health Act
    C. Fair Labor Standards Act
    D. Hazard Communication.

97. If a company employee is earning a salary that is deemed to be excessive when compared to their counterparts of equal ability, their pay rate may be identified as what type of rate?

    A. Red circle
    B. Lump-sum pay
    C. Revenue production
    D. Compensation market pricing.

98. An organization conducts an employee survey and finds that many employees are bored with their jobs, unhappy with their pay, and feel as though they don't get enough vacation time. If the organization's primary goal is to motivate employees, what is the first step that should be taken?

    A. Conduct a survey to determine pay rates and vacation allotments among labor market competitors.
    B. Identify ways in which employees' jobs can be enriched, and implement them.
    C. Give everyone an across-the-board raise and let employees know you will conduct a salary survey to see if further adjustments are needed.
    D. Conduct another employee survey to see if the results are consistent with the results of the first survey.

99. According to OSHA standards, which of the following workplace hazards receives priority when it comes to inspections?

    A. Imminent danger
    B. Employee complaints
    C. Programmed High
    D. Catastrophes and Fatal.

100. According to the FLSA, employers are required to pay nonexempt employees for time spent doing which of the following?

    A. Traveling to and from job sites
    B. Being on-call while at home

C. Sitting around at work, doing something else while waiting for an assignment

D. Company training programs.

101. Finn's boss asked him to put together a list of SMART key performance indicators for their organization, Iron Man, Inc. Which of the following lists correctly identifies SMART indicators?

A. Specific, Measurable, Achievable, Realistic, Timely
B. Solitary, Monetary, Accessible, Realistic, Timely
C. Strategic, Measurable, Authorized, Related, Targeted
D. Strong, Monetary, Achievable, Reactionary, Targeted.

102. Maintaining awareness of opportunities and threats is known as:

A. SWOT analysis
B. Environmental scanning
C. Strategic planning
D. Contingency planning.

103. What is a picture of an organization's financial situation on a specific day (usually the last day of the accounting period)?

A. Profit and loss statement (P&L)
B. Statement of cash flows
C. Product placement
D. Balance sheet.

104. Restricted stock is subject to special SEC regulations before it can ever be sold on the market.

A. True
B. False

105. Of the following, which should be included in a supervisory training program?

    A. Risk management
    B. A rotation through all the business divisions
    C. Conflict resolution skills
    D. Effective employee training.

106. An employee who just turned 18 the day before he was hired a few weeks ago drops a box of materials on his foot, is taken to the emergency room and is diagnosed with several broken bones. Which of the following has to happen?

    A. OSHA must be notified within 8 hours
    B. The OSHA Form 300 must be completed within six working days.
    C. The OSHA Form 301 must be completed and posted within seven calendar days of the date on which the employer learns of the work-related injury or illness.
    D. The OSHA Form 300A must be completed within seven calendar days of the work-related injury or illness.

107. A European woman applies for a job with an airline company. The job requires the employee to speak French. Which of the following questions can be asked during the interview?

    A. Where were you born?
    B. When were you born?
    C. Are you a citizen of another country?
    D. Do you speak French?

108. Which of the following is not an element of a SMART goal?

    A. Measurable
    B. Scientific
    C. Realistic
    D. Timed

109. Howard is a division manager at Here Comes the Sun, where you are the HR representative. Howard is extremely frustrated with the new performance appraisal system in which all employees are ranked in comparison to each other; some employees must be rated low, even if their performance is objectively good. What type of performance appraisal system are you using at Here Comes the Sun?

    A. Job ranking
    B. Forced distribution
    C. Forced comparison
    D. Narrative method.

110. During the evaluation phase, which type of evaluation method focuses upon how well an employee's training actually resulted in new competencies and skills related to the position?

    A. Learning
    B. Results
    C. Reaction
    D. Behavior.

111. A manager who you know fairly well, and with whom you have a good working relationship, leaves a voicemail message for you asking you to please call her back about a benefits question. You return her call, and she comes down to your office to speak with you in person. She explains that her former assistant, who left nearly a year and a half ago to go back to college, is about to run out of COBRA. She explains to you that he still is one semester away from earning his degree and can't get decent health insurance through the college plan. She asks if you wouldn't mind leaving him on COBRA, just for a few more months. You know that you've got to formulate a response that accomplishes a number of things, including providing accurate facts. Which of the following facts would be the most appropriate to share?

    A. You inform the manager that, under COBRA, former employees who are full-time students at the time that COBRA runs out are entitled to an extension for as long as the former employee remains a full-time student (up to 18 months).

B. You inform the manager that although COBRA only requires an employer to continue benefits coverage for 18 months, the employer has the option to extend COBRA benefits for an additional 18 months.

C. You inform the manager that COBRA can be continued for another 18 months, as long as the employee pays the company 110% of the monthly premium costs.

D. You inform the employee that COBRA cannot be continued beyond 18 months in this particular situation, but there are other situations that would warrant an extension and that you would be happy to share that information with her.

112. What does a SWOT analysis look at in an organization?

A. Strengths, weaknesses, opportunities, and threats
B. Strategy, workforce, occupational hazards, and total income
C. Strategic management, workforce politics, occupational hazards, and threats
D. Strengths, weaknesses, organization culture, and turnover rate.

113. Which of the following attempts to add diversity to a workforce or increase the effectiveness of an already diverse workforce?

A. Diversity training
B. Professional development
C. Diversity initiative
D. Human resource information system.

114. In the acronym SMART, M stands for

A. Marketable
B. Meaningful
C. Measurable
D. Motivational.

115. The function of marketing is often described by the four P's. Which of the following sets is the four P's?

    A. Price, product, placement, and promotion
    B. Pressure, position, product, and professional
    C. Price, position, product, and promotion
    D. Pacify, perks, placement, and promotion.

116. All the following are valuable guidelines for managing a vendor and a relationship with a vendor except:

    A. Giving the vendor constructive and positive feedback.
    B. Setting clear and reasonable expectations.
    C. Converting full-time vendors from independent contracts to employees to foster greater esprit de corps.
    D. Incorporating upside potential and downside risk into your negotiated agreements with vendors.

117. You've been asked to make a recommendation relative to a new HRIS for your organization, and you need to collect information to assist you in formulating that recommendation. During the HRIS needs assessment, it would be important for you to ask all the following questions except

    A. To what degree are current employees familiar with the new system?
    B. What financial resources can you commit to purchasing and implementing the system?
    C. What human and capital resources will be required to support the implementation of the system?
    D. What financial, human, and capital resources will be required to support and maintain the system?

118. Environmental scanning identifies _____ opportunities and threats.

    A. Regulatory
    B. Internal
    C. External

D. Market.

119. What is an organizational structure that defines departments by what services they contribute to the organization's overall mission?

   A. Functional
   B. Service-based
   C. Mission-based
   D. Decentralized.

120. An organization's four stages are:

   A. Launch, Investment, Growth, Decline
   B. Formation, Growth, Maturity, Stagnation
   C. Introduction, Growth, Maturity, Decline
   D. Startup, Investment, Growth, Sale.

121. Human capital is the combined _____, _____, and _____ of a company's employees.

   A. Knowledge, skills, experience
   B. Education, experience, salary
   C. Knowledge, education, experience
   D. Knowledge, experience, salary.

122. Which of the following is not part of a PERT chart?

   A. Technique
   B. Plan
   C. Evaluation
   D. Review.

123. Gross profit margin measures the difference between what it costs to _____ a product and the selling price.

   A. Research, produce, and market
   B. Market.

C. Produce.

D. Research.

124. A regulation is a rule or order issued by a government agency which _____ has the force or law.

   A. Often

   B. Never

   C. Rarely

   D. Always.

125. An HR audit measures which of the following?

   A. Regulatory compliance

   B. Retention practices

   C. HR programs & positions

   D. Hiring practices.

126. The number of members of an organization that have to be present before official business may be conducted is called a:

   A. Majority

   B. Quorum

   C. Representation

   D. Super majority.

127. Incremental budgeting uses a _____ budget as the basis for the allocation of funds.

   A. An estimated

   B. Zero-based

   C. Prior

   D. Static.

128. A _____ is the expected distribution given a random sampling of people across a large population.

    A. An algorithmic distribution
    B. Uniform distribution
    C. Normal distribution
    D. Stochastic distribution.

129. Which of the following is a human resources function that identifies organizational human capital needs and attempts to provide an adequate supply of qualified individuals for jobs in an organization?

    A. Forecasting
    B. Staffing
    C. Hiring
    D. Retention.

130. Which of the following refers to the link between a selection device and job performance?

    A. Predictive validity
    B. Content validity
    C. Criterion-related validity
    D. Construct validity.

131. What type of interview focuses on how the applicant previously handled real work situations?

    A. An informational interview
    B. Situational interview
    C. Case interview
    D. Behavioral interview.

132. Which of the following is not utilized in judgmental forecasts?

    A. Nominal group technique
    B. Industry trends

C. Managerial estimates

D. Delphi technique

133. What type of interview focuses on how an applicant would handle hypothetical real work situations?

A. An informational interview

B. Case interview

C. Behavioral interview

D. Situational interview.

134. The Workers Adjustment and Restraining Notification Act (WARN) requires some employers to give a minimum of _____ days' notice if a plant is going to close or if mass layoffs will occur.

A. 60

B. 120

C. 90

D. 30.

135. An employer makes working conditions so intolerable that an employee has no choice but to resign. This is called:

A. Constructive discharge

B. S force out

C. Restrictive retention

D. Unfair working conditions.

136. Yield ratios can help quantify:

A. An organizational accountability

B. Employee engagement

C. Recruitment efforts

D. Retention efforts.

137. A job group analysis is part of a(n):

    A. Compensation study.
    B. Workforce analysis
    C. Benefits plan
    D. Affirmative action plan.

138. Which of the following is a type of evidence that can be gathered to defend the use of one test for predicting an outcome related to another test taken at the same time?

    A. Predictive validity
    B. Construct validity
    C. Convergent validity
    D. Concurrent validity

139. Which of the following protects the privacy of e-mail in storage?

    A. USA Patriot act
    B. Wiretap act
    C. Electronic communications privacy act
    D. Stored communications act.

140. Which OSHA standard protects employees from the environmental, process, chemical, mechanical, or radiological hazards capable of causing injury or impairment and sets criteria for acceptable equipment designs?

    A. Personal protective equipment standard
    B. Process safety management standard
    C. Hazard communication standard
    D. Occupational safety and health standard

141. Which act sets forth provisions for access, use, disclosure, interception, and privacy protections of electronic communications?

    A. USA Patriot act
    B. Wiretap Act

C. Electronic Communications Privacy Act.

D. Stored Communications Act.

142. Any deviation from an acceptable standard is:

A. A risk

B. An incident

C. A hazard

D. A policy violation

143. A violation of an OSHA standard that is considered intentional is called:

A. Less-than-serious

B. Serious

C. Willful

D. Purposeful

144. Which of the following is not a requirement of the OSHA hazard communication standard?

A. Labeling of hazardous chemicals

B. Hazardous chemical cleanup training

C. New employee orientation

D. MSDS

145. Which act prohibits the interception of e-mails in transmission?

A. USA Patriot Act

B. Electronic Communications Privacy Act

C. Stored Communications Act

D. Wiretap Act

146. A modified-duty program applies to employees who are:

A. Pending termination

B. In-training

C. Working part-time

D. Injured or ill

147. Material Safety Data Sheets (MSDS) must be provided by:

    A. The American Chemical Association (ACA)
    B. Chemical manufacturers
    C. Employers
    D. OSHA

148. The key difference between an occupational illness and an occupational injury is the:

    A. Job classification of the affected employee
    B. OSHA classification of the hazard
    C. Amount of recovery time
    D. Length of exposure to the hazard

149. Which of the following is used as a supplemental record that covers the details of each occupational injury and illness?

    A. OSHA Form 300
    B. OSHA Form 300A
    C. OSHA Form 301
    D. OSHA Form 301A

150. Which of the following prohibits discrimination against individuals on the basis of their genetic information?

    A. ADA
    B. FLSA
    C. GINA
    D. OSHA

151. Which of these employers does the Fair Labor Standards Act not cover?

    A. A local fire department
    B. An elementary school

C. A store with $250,000 in sales

D. A nursing home

152. A point-of-service plan (POS) is a type of managed care plan that is a hybrid of which of the following types of plans?

A. PPO and IRA

B. HSA and PPO

C. HMO and HSA

D. HMO and PPO

153. To qualify for special tax treatment, a health savings account (HSA) for a single person must have a deductible of at least _____ and out-of-pocket limits of no more than _____.

A. $1,200, $5,950

B. $2,400, $5,950

C. $1,200, $11,900

D. $2,400, $11,900

154. When an organization's pay rates are at least equal to market rates there is:

A. An external equity

B. Wage parity

C. Internal equity

D. A prevailing wage

155. An employee experiences a qualifying event. This will impact his or her:

A. Eligibility for additional paid leave

B. Compensation

C. Group healthcare coverage

D. Eligibility for retirement

156. What act provides individuals and dependents who may lose medical coverage with the opportunity to pay to continue coverage?

    A. EPA
    B. UCA
    C. COBRA
    D. Sarbanes Oxley

157. What is the name of the act that defines what is included as hours worked and is therefore compensable and a factor in calculating overtime?

    A. A Portal-to-Portal Act
    B. Sarbanes Oxley Act
    C. Service Contract Act
    D. Davis-Bacon Act

158. The Revenue Act created:

    A. 401(k) plans.
    B. 403(b) plans.
    C. Health savings accounts.
    D. Flexible spending accounts.

159. When employees feel that performance or job differences result in corresponding differences in pay rates it's called:

    A. Internal equity.
    B. Organizational Equity.
    C. Compensation equity.
    D. External equity.

160. Pay based on when or where an employee works is called:

    A. Differential pay
    B. Variant pay
    C. Hourly pay
    D. Overtime pay

161. Which of the following is not one of the obstacles to learning?

    A. Lack of process
    B. Lack of trust
    C. Peer group pressure
    D. Low tolerance for change

162. Career development consists of career _____ and career _____.

    A. Planning, management
    B. Education, planning
    C. Planning, maintenance
    D. Education, management

163. Successful orientation programs include which of the following?

    A. One-day vs. multi-day training
    B. Use of orientation checklists
    C. Massive delivery of information
    D. Passive participation

164. Which of the following is not a learning style?

    A. Visual
    B. Auditory
    C. Kinesthetic
    D. Artificial

165. He was one of the first to write about the cost of poor quality and developed a "trilogy" approach to cross-functional management.

    A. Blake Mouton
    B. Edwards Deming
    C. Philip B. Crosby
    D. Joseph J. Juran.

166. Systems theory focuses on improving system:

    A. Inputs
    B. Teamwork
    C. Outputs
    D. Processes.

167. What are intervention strategies that deal with work relationships between employees?

    A. Team-based
    B. Structural
    C. Interpersonal
    D. Communicative

168. Finding and eliminating problems that interfere with quality and creating an environment that is conducive to creativity are two benefits of:

    A. A total quality management (TQM) system
    B. Organizational learning
    C. Organizational development
    D. Team building

169. Equity theory is based on the belief that people want to be:

    A. Treated fairly
    B. Given preferential treatment
    C. Recognized for their work
    D. Well compensated.

170. Copyright protection covers the life of the author plus how many years

    A. 50
    B. 10
    C. 70
    D. 60

171. Which of the following is not a type of organizational development intervention?

    A. Compensation studies
    B. Quality initiatives
    C. Team building
    D. Diversity programs

172. An agency shop clause governs:

    A. Unions
    B. Contractors
    C. Hourly employees
    D. Exempt employees

173. What is a planned and orderly attempt to link the shared interests of the employee and the organization for their mutual benefit called?

    A. On-boarding
    B. Employee participation program
    C. Team building
    D. Employee involvement

174. The duty of fair representation requires that _____ act fairly on behalf of employees.

    A. NLRB
    B. Unions
    C. Local governments
    D. Employers

175. Union security clauses are designed to protect:

    A. Union employees
    B. Unions
    C. Employers
    D. Union jobs.

176. Which federal agency is responsible for enforcing anti-discrimination laws and handling charges?

    A. OSHA
    B. EEOC
    C. NLRB
    D. Department of Justice.

Answer Key

Q.	1	2	3	4	5	6	7	8	9	10	11	12	13	14	15	16
A.	C	B	A	C	A	B	A	D	D	C	B	A	A	B	A	B

Q.	17	18	19	20	21	22	23	24	25	26	27	28	29	30	31	32
A.	A	A	B	C	D	A	A	C	C	A	A	A	C	A	B	C

Q.	33	34	35	36	37	38	39	40	41	42	43	44	45	46	47	48
A.	A	D	A	C	C	A	A	A	A	B	B	A	B	C	C	D

Q.	49	50	51	52	53	54	55	56	57	58	59	60	61	62	63	64
A.	D	C	A	B	B	B	C	D	B	B	C	C	A	A	A	B

Q.	65	66	67	68	69	70	71	72	73	74	75	76	77	78	79	80
A.	C	D	A	B	D	A	A	C	D	B	B	A	B	C	D	B

Q.	81	82	83	84	85	86	87	88	89	90	91	92	93	94	95	96
A.	A	A	B	D	C	B	D	B	B	B	C	B	A	C	A	C

Q.	97	98	99	100	101	102	103	104	105	106	107	108	109	110	111	112
A.	A	A	A	C	A	B	D	A	C	B	D	B	B	A	D	A

Q.	113	114	115	116	117	118	119	120	121	122	123	124	125	126	127	128
A.	C	C	A	C	A	C	A	C	A	B	C	A	A	B	C	C

Q.	129	130	131	132	133	134	135	136	137	138	139	140	141	142	143	144
A.	B	C	D	B	D	A	A	C	D	D	D	A	C	B	C	B

Q.	145	146	147	148	149	150	151	152	153	154	155	156	157	158	159	160
A.	D	D	B	D	C	C	C	D	A	A	C	C	A	A	A	A

Q.	161	162	163	164	165	166	167	168	169	170	171	172	173	174	175	176
A.	A	A	B	D	D	D	C	A	A	C	A	A	D	B	B	B

Answer Explanations

1. C: The list of employees who are eligible to vote in the union election is called the Excelsior List based on the outcome of the lawsuit Excelsior Underwear, Inc. v. NLRB in 1996.

2. B: The client is not one of the four components of the HR Impact Model. The four components are the catalyst, consultation, policies and procedures, and programs and processes.

3. A. Bumping is when a senior employee's position is being eliminated and she elects to move to a less senior position and force a less senior worker out of employment.

4. C. The technical term of arbitration, based on the interpretation of the language of the contract, is called a decision.

5. A. In Washington versus Davis, two African Americans were denied positions at the Washington DC police department because of their performance on a job-related test. The US Supreme Court ruled against the plaintiffs and deemed that the test did not violate the due process clause.

6. B. The plan administrator is required to provide participants, at no cost, with plan information about the features and funding of the plan.

7. A is an example of disparate treatment. Fran has treated this applicant differently than the other applicants because the person says he speaks Spanish.

8. D. An on-site cafeteria is an example of a non-monetary reward.

9. D. The point factor technique identifies points of performance based on importance to the organization. Within each point, levels of performance are created. Both levels and points are then weighted based on most important to least important, to determine the overall performance of each employee.

10. C. Fair Pay determines that a person earning $100,000 or more is considered to be highly compensated.

11. B. Clearly outlining to each new employee what they are responsible for can help your business in the long run.

12. A. An employee opinion survey or poll gives HR professionals the chance to learn directly about where the organization is doing well and where further intervention is needed.

13. A. The more a company's employees feel involved in the decision-making processes, the more empowered and well-treated they would feel. This would, in turn, enhance their commitment and loyalty to the organization.

14. B. If there is no or insufficient evidence of the alleged misconduct, initiating a disciplinary procedure would be unfair to the accused and could lead to a waste of resources.

15. A. Unlike arbitration, where the process of settlement is dictated by an arbiter, mediation is more informal, as the third party merely helps the parties settle their differences.

16. B. An arbitral process ends with a decision to dictate the terms of the settlement. An arbitral decision is often enforced by the law courts.

17. A. Sidestepping a union rep is legally recognized as evidence of bad faith on the part of management in the collective bargaining process.

18. A. To certify or decertify a union, the employees must first file an RD petition with the National Labor Relations Board (NLRB). If 30 percent of the staff in the bargaining unit endorse the petition, the NLRB would conduct a hearing and call for votes to complete the process.

19. B. Leadership initiatives and training on unfair labor practices teach managers how their actions and words daily have a big impact on fostering a workplace free of the need for unions.

20.   C. Employees who feel fairly treated and supported will be more committed to the mission of their employers.

21.   D. If an employee is treated poorly, they would have no reason to take part in staff training programs to advance the goals of their abusive managers.

22.   A. The more involved employees feel in proposed work programs, the more invested and engaged they would become. Also, as an HR professional, you would be able to curate programs more suited to the staff's pain points with their input.

23.   A. Top-down communication is a highly effective communication technique for corporations where information is passed down from senior leadership across the organization.

24.   A is legally recognized as an abnormal health condition brought on by exposure to work-related environmental factors.

25.   A. OSHA is the federal statute that clearly and thoroughly regulates workplace safety and health.

26.   A. This is the initial course of action recognized by the relevant statute in such a situation. There is no need to alert OSHA unless the injury involves at least three employees and the nature of the injury resulted in their hospitalization.

27.   A. Unless the drinking problem has been recognized by the employee's teammates and persisted for a while, symptoms such as lateness and lack of concentration, could have well been brought on by other behavioral challenges.

28.   A. Employers with federal contracts or grants are mandated to maintain a drug-free workplace.

29.   C is a negative and discriminatory measure prohibited by labor laws.

30. A. As soon as an OSHA inspector arrives at your organization, your first responsibility is to confirm that they are who they claim to be.

31. B. Asbestosis is a serious lung disease. It is often difficult to detect and treat early on, as its symptoms can lie dormant for many years.

32. C. Even though regional laws differ, it is against the law for employers in the United States to either refuse to hire or fire a worker for using any kind of tobacco product outside of work hours or off company property.

33. A. Potential security threats in the foreign countries they are posted to are a unique safety problem for expatriates.

34. D. If any member of staff is brave enough to tell you about such a problem, as the HR professional, how you react is very important. The person should be reassured that their career and your opinion of them have not been negatively affected, even as you figure out how this might affect other employees.

35. A. This is a good example of a positive reinforcement strategy.

36. C is the precise length of days specified in the WARN Act for a written warning to be issued by such a company.

37. C. The Occupational Safety and Health Standards was the first piece of legislation from the correction option to specify workplace safety requirements.

38. A is the method that fits this definition the best.

39. A, C, and D is the combination that best describes the advantages of gainsharing programs.

40. A. A is the only legally acceptable question from the correction options to be asked in an interview.

41. A. This is the period stipulated for employers to submit an eligibility form to verify a potential employee's right to work in the US.

42. B. SWOT is an analysis that can be used to determine the strengths, weaknesses, opportunities, and threats.

43. B. There are four types of validity that HR professionals should be familiar with: content validity, criterion-related validity, construct validity, and predictive validity. There is no such category as professional validity.

44. A. The EEO-4 Report, formally known as the state and local government report, is collected on odd years.

45. B. HR Professionals want to be both effective and efficient, but there is a difference. Efficiency is doing things right. Effectiveness is doing the right things.

46. C. The Railway Labor Act was a critical win for the management, in that it helped keep trains, and later airlines, from striking - to disrupt the travel of citizens. The act was created to keep the trains moving - with a few exceptions, such as safety.

47. C. Third-party investigators. FACT Act Eliminates Need for Prior Consent When Third Parties Conduct Workplace Investigations.

48. D. TIPS is an acronym used by many labor management attorneys and consultants that covers most of the unfair labor practice pitfalls a supervisor can run into. It stands for (don't) Threaten, Interrogate, Promise, or Spy.

49. D. Union security clauses are provisions in a collective bargaining agreement designed to protect the institutional authority or survival of the union.

50. C. The Civil Service Reform Act extended collective bargaining rights to federal employees.

51. A. Defamation is injuring someone's reputation by making a false and

malicious statement. Defamation may be spoken (slander) or written (libel).

52.   B. A closed shop clause states that union membership is a condition of hiring is illegal (except in the construction industry).

53.   B. Employment-at-will is a common-law principle stating that employers have the right to hire, fire, demote, and promote whomever they choose for any reason unless there is a law or contract to the contrary and that employees have the right to quit a job at any time.

54.   B. The process of sending employees abroad and supporting their ability to adapt to cultural changes and complete their international assignments is called expatriation.

55.   C. Career planning focuses on the needs of employees. The goal is to take care of employee career needs and desires to motivate employees and allow them to achieve their full potential. The belief is that in doing so, employees will become more productive, remain happy, and ultimately work harder and longer for the organization.

56.   D. A yellow dog contract is the term for an agreement between management and a potential employee to offer the potential employee a job as long as they agree not to join a union. Before 1932, when yellow dog contracts were outlawed under the Norris-LaGuardia Act, these contracts were used widely to prevent the formation of unions within companies.

57.   B. Excluding statements relative to how the code will be implemented and upheld greatly diminishes the likelihood that the code will be effective. Doing so, in effect, robs the code of teeth.

58.   B. Of the risk management techniques, avoidance is defined as an act of stopping or not attempting a business activity that may or may not result in some kind of loss.

59.   C. The phrase "third-party contract" always refers to a situation in which

someone is involved in a business transaction, deal, or mediation, and they are not otherwise directly involved with the situation.

60. C. Risk management is the correct term for the process of identifying risks and taking effective steps to minimize them.

61. A. In this situation, Sione is nonexempt, based on the salary requirements. According to the FLSA, an employee in any given business must be classified as either exempt or nonexempt. To be exempt, an employee must be paid a salary of at least $23,660 per year. An employee who is entitled to hourly pay (at minimum wage or above), overtime, and protections under child labor and equal pay, that employee is considered to be non-exempt.

62. A. The Means of Egress standard provides guidelines for preparing a corporate emergency action plan and creates specifications for unobstructed means of exit from any point in a company's building.

63. A. A statistical HR measurement that assesses productivity is revenue per employee. Using the equation of the company's net income divided by the number of employees, the company can compare the resulting number with similar companies. Although the higher the number the better in a general sense, there are no rules about what, exactly, constitutes a good level of income per employee.

64. B. The Drug Free Workplace Act allows employers to follow drug testing and drug-free workplace policies to ensure a healthy workplace for all.

65. C. Offshoring refers to the process of outsourcing to third-party providers whose operations are based overseas.

66. D. Blake-Mouton's situational leadership theory builds on Hersey and Blanchard's model. It identifies "impoverished managers" as those who delegate responsibility, then demonstrates no real concern for either people or task/production. This model uses a nine-point scale along each axis.

67. A. A PEST analysis, used during the strategic planning process, refers

to the "Political, Economic, Social, and Technological" factors that may affect the overall strategy of an organization.

68. B. The McDonnell-Douglas Corp v. Green was a United States Supreme Court case that established disparate treatment and led to the amendment of Title VII of the Civil Rights Act of 1964. Under Title VII, the Equal Employment Opportunity Commission is responsible for investigating possible claims of discrimination based on race, color, religion, sex, or national origin.

69. D. The Davis-Bacon act requires that companies with federal construction contracts must pay their laborers and mechanics the standard wage of employees in the geographic area in which the work is being performed.

70. A. This employee is trying to avoid negative consequences that could result from revealing proprietary information.

71. A. A mission statement describes what an organization does and how that is different from what other organizations may do. It provides a general framework in which the overall strategy of the country is formed.

72. C. HR adds value to this process by asking questions that help us ascertain the underlying problems and distinguish problems from symptoms.

73. D. Needs assessment and needs analysis are generally used interchangeably to describe methods for obtaining any information that may be necessary to make decisions that will best allow the organization to accomplish its goals. In human resources, they are often used for training and development, staffing projecting, budgets, and benefit planning.

74. B. An Ishikawa diagram is the best quality tool for gathering information about a specific problem because it shows the particular causes of a business event.

75. B. A serious violation is the second level of violation and occurs when there is a substantial probability of death or serious physical harm. Willful violations are done intentionally or with "plain indifference" to

the requirements and have the potential for serious harm or injury. Repeat violations are violations for which an employer has been previously cited and has recurred. De-minimus violations are unlikely to cause serious harm or injury.

76. A. Esteem is the second highest need on Maslow's hierarchy. Although it could be argued that a living wage falls under the category of basic physical needs, it is not - by definition - the same as basic physical needs. In part, this is because the concept of a living wage did not exist when Maslow developed his hierarchy. Also, earning a living wage does not ensure that all the dimensions of a person's basic physical needs will be met.

77. B. According to the FLSA, an employee in any given business must be classified as either exempt or nonexempt. In order to be exempt, an employee must be paid a salary of at least $23,660 per year. An employee who is entitled to hourly pay (at minimum wage or above), overtime, and protections under child labor and equal pay, that employee is considered to be non-exempt.

78. C. Rational is not one of the elements of a SMART goal. A SMART goal is specific, measurable, achievable, realistic, and time-based.

79. D. all them will need to be addressed in a needs analysis to select an HRIS. Only once these questions are asked can research begin on a system that will effectively meet the company's needs.

80. B. If an employee so chooses, they can petition the NLRB to decertify the union. In this case, the employee would have to provide evidence that at least 30% of the union supports the decertification.

81. A. First, it is important for the employee to understand how the process works, so it is appropriate to share that information with her. You don't need to go into all those reasons with the employee. Although the factual information at the beginning of Option B is correct, there are many reasons why you should not falsify the termination code. As HR, your role is to be a "truth advocate," not an employee advocate, and in truth the employee wasn't laid off.

82.   A. Human relations is the concept that recognized that businesses are social organizations and economic systems and recognized that employee productivity was directly related to job satisfaction.

83.   B. A serious violation is one that the employer either knew about or should have known about. "Serious" violations are issued by OSHA, and not by the Department of Justice. A serious violation is likely to result in death or serious injury, so option C is not possible. Again, "serious" violations are issued only by OSHA, and not by the EEOC or any other government body, so option D is not possible.

84.   D. A lockout refers to a work stoppage during which an employer will physically prevent employees from working. Although employers may sometimes impose a lockdown in protest against slowdowns, typically they are due to issues with unions and negotiations.

85.   C. Abraham Maslow, a behavioral scientist, developed the Hierarchy of Needs in 1954. In this theory, it explains all the myriad needs that people meet through a successful and satisfying work life: physiological needs (like food and shelter), safety needs, social needs, esteem needs, and needs for self-actualization.

86.   B. Featherbedding is the practice of hiring more workers than is needed to perform a job. It can also describe work procedures that appear to be pointless or unnecessarily complicated, simply to employ additional workers. The Taft-Hartley Act explicitly prohibits this action.

87.   D. Observing the incumbent performing the work is necessary to determine whether there is an ergonomic hazard in the job.

88.   B. The 1936 Walsh-Healey Act is a federal law that protects the employees of government contractors who have holdings over $10,000. Under the act, which was part of the New Deal, the employees were guaranteed overtime if they worked more than eight hours a day or 30 hours a week, set the minimum age, and set basic standards for child labor laws.

89.   B. Copyright is the set of exclusive rights that are granted to the creator of

original creative works under United States law. Under the law, materials are protected as soon as they are first saved electronically or printed and the copyright lasts for a certain period (which varies, depending upon the work, medium, etc.), after which the work enters the public domain.

90. B. The Expectancy Theory, developed by Victor Vroom in 1964, surmises that people are motivated by the reward they will receive when they succeed at a task. The employee will then calculate the level of effort they are required to put in to achieve that goal.

91. C. Constructive discharge (also called constructive dismissal) occurs when an employee resigns because of poor behavior by their employer. The resigning employee must prove that the conduct was unlawful or a breach of contract. Usually, a constructive dismissal allows the employee to make legal claims against the employer.

92. B. This dimension of leadership relates to the dimensions of leadership that speak specifically to ensuring that employees successfully perform the work associated with the position.

93. A. In this case, Eliza is using the Delphi technique. The most important thing to remember about the Delphi technique is its focus on keeping opinions and ideas anonymous. The advantage of this is that it focuses upon the quality of the information-not who is saying it.

94. C. A positively accelerated learning curve initially begins slowly, with smaller learning increments, but increases in pace and with larger increments as learning proceeds. The positively accelerating learning curve typically corresponds to when a learner is mastering new and different aspects of a process or task. During this time, the worker will usually learn slowly and in small increments.

95. A. Vestibule training allows new or inexperienced workers to use any job equipment that either requires a certain level of speed or is hazardous. Such training would be appropriate for cashiers, construction workers, tool and die makers, etc.

96.   C. The Fair Labor Standards Act (FLSA) defines a list of jobs that are not suitable for children between the ages of 16 and 18. The Mine Safety and Health Act ensured the safety of workers in coal and other mines. The Occupational Safety and Health Act sets safety standards for all industries. The Hazard Communication Standard requires employers to provide employees with information about physical and health hazards related to the use of any chemicals in the workplace.

97.   A. A red circle rate occurs when a company employee is determined to be earning a salary that is above the maximum range for a job or when it is deemed excessive when compared to their peers.

98.   A. According to Herzberg's Motivation-Hygiene theory, motivation factors will have a positive impact on an employee's motivation level if and only if hygiene factors are acceptable. It's important to deal first with hygiene factors to ensure that motivation factors will have a positive impact.

99.   A. According to OSHA standards, workplace hazards deemed as being in "imminent danger" receive top priority for inspections. Although you may want to assume that catastrophes and fatal incidents would receive a higher priority, because they have already occurred, there is little that OSHA can do at that point. From their standpoint, it is better to focus on and stop any potential catastrophes from happening.

100. C. According to the FLSA, employers are required to pay nonexempt employees for time spent sitting around at work, doing something else while waiting for an assignment.

101. A. SMART indicators are Specific, Measurable, Achievable, Realistic, and Timely.

102. B. Environmental scanning refers to the process of maintaining an awareness of opportunities and threats. Although maintaining awareness of opportunities and threats is part of the SWOT analysis, this also incorporates maintaining awareness of strengths and weaknesses. A SWOT analysis is an essential part of strategic planning, but it does not encompass everything that is involved in strategic planning. Although an organization's

awareness of threats is likely to highlight the need for contingency planning, those two concepts are synonymous.

103. D. The balance sheet is a general picture of an organization's financial situation on a specific day (usually the last day of the accounting period). It is a very useful tool for summarizing financial information and the result of normal business activity. Typical types of information on the organization's balance sheet are the company's assets, liabilities, and equity.

104. A. Restricted stock is subject to special SEC regulations before it can ever be sold on the market. Typically, restricted stock is given as a reward to insiders after an acquisition or a merger. Doing so will prevent an adverse impact on the market price of the stock, as it will be required that stockholders actually hold on to the stock for a prescribed period before they may sell it publicly.

105. C. Of the items listed, conflict resolution skills should be included in a supervisory training program. Typically, supervisory training involves topics that deal directly with employee interaction and management.

106. B. The OSHA Form 300 must be completed within six working days. OSHA must be notified within 8 hours only in the event of a death or the inpatient hospitalization of three or more employees. The OSHA form 301 requires a detailed account of each work-related injury or accident. Although it must be completed within seven calendar days, it is not posted. The OSHA Form 300A is a summary report of all work-related injuries and illnesses that take place in a calendar year and therefore cannot be completed until after the end of the year.

107. D. The only interview questions that are allowed are those that specifically relate to job qualifications. Personal questions about health, country of origin, family status, religion, etc. are all considered to be inappropriate.

108. B. Scientific is not one of the elements of a SMART goal. Remember that a SMART goal is specific, measurable, action-oriented, realistic, and time-based.

109. B. In the forced distribution method (also known as forced ranking), the managers are compelled to force employee performance into a bell-curve system, with a top 10%, next 35%, next 45%, and the bottom 10%. In this system, most employees will fall into the middle of the performance spectrum.

110. A. There are four standard methods that businesses use to evaluate employees and their respective training: learning, behavior, reaction and results. The learning method focuses upon how well an employee's training actually resulted in learning new competencies and skills; the reaction method looks at participant reactions to training; the behavior method quantifies on-the-job behavior modifications that have resulted from training; and the results method looks at the overall results of the organization. Typically, the results method is thought of as the most valuable method for a company.

111. D. According to the facts you have been given, COBRA can't be extended, but it's also true that there may be other facts of which you're not aware. You should be helpful, factual, and accurate.

112. A. A SWOT analysis looks at the strengths, weaknesses, opportunities, and threats to an organization. Strengths and weaknesses are typically viewed as internal factors that either lead to or deter from a company's success. Opportunities and threats, while sometimes internal, are typically external factors that may affect an organization's overall strategic plan.

113. C. A diversity initiative is typically a company-wide objective to either add diversity to the company's workforce or to expand upon the effectiveness of the company's already diverse workforce. Typically, the initiative will begin with a meeting to discuss the benefits of corporate diversity and an open discussion about any of the changes occurring within the company.

114. C. Objectives, whether related to performance management or any other HRD initiative, must be measurable. Although goals should be marketable, to the degree that they relate to the overarching objectives of the organization and are, therefore, hopefully widely embraced, marketability

is not one of the key driving forces behind goal setting. Options B and D are not the best for similar responses.

115.   A. In marketing, the four Ps are price, product, placement, and promotion. The "four Ps" concept to describe marketing is commonly used in most textbooks and classes and was proposed by a very prominent marketer, E. Jerome McCarthy, in 1960.

116.   C. Vendors, by definition, are not employees. Whether to classify individuals as employees or contractors is a legal determination, not an emotional or psychological one.

117.   A. The degree to which current employees are familiar with the new system is relatively unimportant as long as communication is effective, training is provided, and support is available.

118.   C. Environmental scanning is a process that surveys and interprets relevant data to identify external opportunities and threats.

119.   A. A functional structure is an organizational structure that defines departments by what services they contribute to the organization's overall mission.

120.   C. An organization's four stages are Introduction, Growth, Maturity, Decline (IGMD).

121.   A. Human capital (KSE) is the combined knowledge, skills, and experience of a company's employees.

122.   B. A program (or project) evaluation and review technique (PERT) chart is a project management tool used to schedule, organize, and coordinate tasks within a project.

123.   C. Gross profit margin measures the difference between what it costs to produce a product and the selling price.

124.   A. A regulation is a rule or order issued by a government agency that often has the force of law.

125. A. An HR audit is a process to measure the effectiveness and efficiency of HR programs & positions.

126. B. A quorum is the number of members of an organization that have to be present before official business may be conducted.

127. C. Incremental budgeting is a form of budgeting in which the prior budget is the basis for the allocation of funds

128. C. A normal distribution is an expected distribution given a random sampling of people across a large population.

129. B. Staffing is a human resources function that identifies organizational human capital needs and attempts to provide an adequate supply of qualified individuals for jobs in an organization.

130. C. Criterion-related validity refers to the link between a selection device and job performance.

131. D. A behavioral interview focuses on how the applicant previously handled actual work situations. (The difference between a behavioral interview and a situational interview is that a behavioral interview focuses on past performance while a situational interview focuses on future performance.)

132. B. Judgmental forecasts use information from the past and present to predict future conditions and use managerial estimates, the Delphi technique, and the nominal group technique.

133. D. A situational interview focuses on how an applicant would handle hypothetical actual work situations. (The difference between a situational interview and a behavioral interview is that a situational interview focuses on future performance while a behavioral interview focuses on past performance.)

134. A. The Workers Adjustment and Restraining Notification Act (WARN) requires some employers to give a minimum of 60 days' notice if a plant is going to close or if mass layoffs will occur.

135. A. Constructive discharge occurs when an employer makes working conditions so intolerable that an employee has no choice but to resign.

136. C. A yield ratio reflects the percentage of job candidates at the beginning of a step in the recruitment/selection process who move on to the next step in that process and can help quantify recruitment efforts.

137. D. A job group analysis is part of an affirmative action plan that lists all job titles that comprise each job group having similar content and responsibilities, wage rates, and opportunities for advancement.

138. D. Concurrent validity is demonstrated when a test correlates well with a measure that has been validated. The two measures may be for the same construct but are more often used for different, but presumably related, constructs. Concurrent validity contrasts with predictive validity, where one measure occurs earlier and predicts some later measure.

139. D. The stored communications act protects the privacy of e-mail in storage.

140. A. The OSHA personal protective equipment standard protects employees from environmental, process, chemical, mechanical, or radiological hazards capable of causing injury or impairment and sets criteria for acceptable equipment designs.

141. C. The Electronic Communications Privacy Act (ECPA) sets forth provisions for access, use, disclosure, interception, and privacy protections of electronic communications.

142. B. An incident is any deviation from an acceptable standard.

143. C. A willful violation of an OSHA standard is one that is intentional.

144. B. The hazard communication standard (or employee right-to-know law) is an Occupational Safety and Health Administration (OSHA) standard that requires labeling, Material Safety Data Sheets (MSDS), training, orientation for new/transferred employees, and communication programs to inform employees of hazardous chemicals in the workplace.

145. D. The wiretap act prohibits the interception of e-mails in transmission.

146. D. A modified-duty program offers an injured or ill employee a less strenuous job until he or she is fit to return to their regular job.

147. B. Material Safety Data Sheets (MSDS) must be provided by manufacturers for every hazardous substance and employers must evaluate chemicals based on their MSDS and inform employees of hazardous properties.

148. D. An occupational illness is a medical condition or disorder caused by multiple exposures to environmental factors associated with employment, while an occupational injury results from a work-related accident or exposure involving a single incident.

149. C. OSHA Form 301 is used as a supplemental record that covers the details of each occupational injury and illness.

150. C. The Genetic Information Nondiscrimination Act (GINA) prohibits discrimination against individuals because of their genetic information in both employment and health care.

151. C. The Wages and the Fair Labor Standards Act (FLSA) establishes minimum wage, overtime pay, record keeping, and youth employment standards affecting employees in the private sector and in Federal, State, and local governments. FLSA covers employers:

    - with $500,000+ in sales
    - involved in interstate commerce
    - who deal with medical issues
    - are schools
    - are the government

152. D. A point-of-service plan (POS) is a type of managed care plan that is a hybrid of HMO and PPO plans. Like an HMO, participants designate an in-network physician to be their primary care provider. But like a PPO, patients may go outside of the provider network for health care services.

153. A. A health savings account (HSA) is a tax-sheltered savings account that must have a deductible of at least $1,200 single or $2,400 family and out-of-pocket limits of no more than $5,950 single or $11,900 family.

154. A. External equity occurs when an organization's pay rates are at least equal to market rates.

155. C. Under the Consolidated Omnibus Budget Reconciliation Act, a qualifying event is one such as termination for reasons other than gross misconduct that allows employees to continue their group healthcare coverage for a specific period.

156. C. The Consolidated Omnibus Budget Reconciliation Act (COBRA) provides individuals and dependents who may lose medical coverage with the opportunity to pay to continue coverage.

157. A. The Portal to Portal Act defines what is included as hours worked and is, therefore, compensable and a factor in calculating overtime. It includes such items as preparatory/concluding activities, waiting time, meals and breaks, travel time, and on-call/ standby time.

158. A. The Revenue Act added sections 125 and 401(k) to the tax code. Section 125 allows employers to offer employees favorable tax treatment on health and welfare benefits and section 401(k) allows employees to make tax-favored pay deferrals toward retirement savings through payroll deductions.

159. A. Internal equity occurs when employees feel that performance or job differences result in corresponding differences in pay rates. They feel that they are being fairly compensated when compared to others in the workplace.

160. A. Differential (or variable) pay is based on when the employee works (e.g. overtime pay, shift pay differential) or where the employee works.

161. A. Obstacles to learning include low tolerance for change, lack of trust, peer group pressure.

162. A. Career development consists of career planning and career management.

163. B. Successful orientation programs include active rather than passive participation by new employees, orientation spread out over a period of time, use of orientation checklists to ensure that all important material is covered, and avoidance of information overload.

164. D. The seven learning styles are:

- Visual (spatial): You prefer using pictures, images, and spatial understanding.
- Aural (auditory-musical): You prefer using sound and music.
- Verbal (linguistic): You prefer using words, both in speech and writing.
- Physical (kinesthetic): You prefer using your body, hands, and sense of touch.
- Logical (mathematical): You prefer using logic, reasoning, and systems.
- Social (interpersonal): You prefer to learn in groups or with other people.
- Solitary (intrapersonal): You prefer to work alone and use self-study.

165. D. Joseph J. Juran was one of the first to write about the cost of poor quality. This was illustrated by his "Juran trilogy", an approach to cross-functional management, which is composed of three managerial processes: quality planning, quality control, and quality improvement.

166. D. Systems theory is the theory that organizations need to understand the relationship between the input, process, and output components and the environment in which they occur. By doing so, they can improve their processes, making them more efficient and cost-effective

167. C. Interpersonal strategies are intervention strategies that deal with work relationships between employees and are directed at improving interpersonal, inter-group, and infra-group relations.

168. A. The benefits of a total quality management (TQM) system include finding and eliminating problems that interfere with quality, identifying customers and satisfying their needs, eliminating waste, encouraging pride and teamwork, and creating an environment that is conducive to creativity.

169.   A. Equity theory is based on the belief that people want to be treated fairly.

170.   C. Copyright protection covers the life of the author plus 70 years.

171.   A. The four organizational development interventions are team building, flexible work and staffing arrangements, diversity programs, and quality initiatives.

172.   A. An agency shop clause is a provision in a collective bargaining agreement that all employees of the firm (whether members of the union) pay a fixed monthly sum to the union as a condition of employment.

173.   D. A planned and orderly attempt to link the shared interests of the employee and the organization for their mutual benefit is called employee involvement (EI).

174.   B. The duty of fair representation requires that unions act fairly on behalf of the employees they represent in negotiating and administering collective bargaining agreements.

175.   B. Union security clauses are provisions in a collective bargaining agreement designed to protect the institutional authority or survival of the union. An example is a clause that makes union membership or payment of dues compulsory for all employees in a bargaining unit.

176.   B. The Equal Employment Opportunity Commission (EEOC) is a federal agency responsible for enforcing anti-discrimination laws and handling charges.

Free Video Offer!

Thank you for purchasing from Hanley Test Preparation! We're honored to help you prepare for your exam. To show our appreciation, we're offering an Exclusive Test Tips Video.

This video includes multiple strategies that will make you successful on your big exam.

All we ask is that you email us your feedback and describe your experience with our product. Amazing, awful, or just so-so. We want to hear what you have to say!

To get your FREE VIDEO, just send us an email at bonusvideo@hanleytestprep.com with **Free Video** in the subject line and the following information in the body of the email:

- The name of the product you purchased
- Your product rating on a scale of 1-5, with 5 being the highest rating.
- Your feedback about the product.

If you have any questions or concerns, please don't hesitate to contact us at support@hanleytestprep.com

Thanks again!

Final Words

The PHR exam is widely recognized as a benchmark of professional competence in the human resources field. It's difficult to navigate, but I have learned that the key is to study hard and remain gentle with yourself. Remain open and teachable through every step of your journey. You can succeed and, overall, you will become an HR expert for all your troubles. I promise.

If you failed this exam in the past, I hope this book has inspired you to give it another chance. If you are taking this exam for the first time, I hope you learned a thing or two about kick-starting your studies, beginning today.

We will conclude this journey by highlighting the things we learned throughout this book:

- In chapter one, you learned all about the PHR exam, how it works, and the eligibility requirements. We discussed the content outline, and some study habits you can adopt to help you prepare adequately for the exam.
- In chapter two, you learned all about the business management topics helpful in the HR profession. We discussed the organizational structure of companies, regulatory processes, corporate governance, data reporting, risk management, employee communications, and several other business elements of an organization.
- In chapter three, you learned about the best hiring processes to find, attract, and employ top talent for your organization. We discussed the relevant laws, staffing alternatives, interviewing techniques, workforce assessment, and the best ways to assess the effectiveness of a corporation's recruitment efforts.

- In chapter four, we discussed how you can apply and evaluate programs as well as how to provide consultation and data to contribute to a company's learning and development actions.
- In chapter five, you learned how to apply, promote, and manage benefit and compensation programs under all related federal laws.
- In chapter six, we discussed all the ways you can implement, manage, and monitor programs and policies that would legally benefit the employee experience within your organization.
- Chapters seven and eight, we concluded with two full-length practice tests with detailed answers.

Thank you for coming on this journey with me. If this book has helped you in any way, please share your honest reviews on Amazon. I'd love to hear from you.

I wish you the best of luck in your PHR exams.

References

Altadonna, Nathan. (2022, February 19). 13 Types of Change Management Models You Should Know.
https://www.apty.io/blog/organizational-change-management-models

Assignment Help. (n.d). Human Resource Management – Task Analysis.
https://www.assignmenthelp.net/assignment_help/human-resources-task-analysis

Bamboo HR. (2022). Workforce Analysis.
https://www.bamboohr.com/hr-glossary/workforce-analysis/

Betterteam. (2022). Code of Ethics: How to create a code of ethics with a free downloadable template.
https://www.betterteam.com/code-of-ethics

Birches Group. (n.d). Five steps to benchmark your company compensation and benefits.
https://birchesgroup.com/2021/03/11/five-steps-to-benchmark-your-companys-compensation-and-benefits/

Business Balls. (n.d). Kirkpatrick Evaluation Method.
https://www.businessballs.com/training-assessment-and-quality-assurance/kirkpatrick-evaluation-method/

Challenge Consulting. (n.d). Methods of HR Selection Techniques. https://www.challengeconsulting.com.au/announcements/methods-of-hr-selection-techniques/

Chron. (2020, December 10). Examples of compensation policies. https://smallbusiness.chron.com/examples-compensation-policies-11000.html

Cosentino, Jayla. (n.d). How to Conduct an HR Investigation in 7 Steps. https://www.aihr.com/blog/hr-investigation/

Davidson, Morrison. (2021, July 16). Different Types of Pay Structures. https://www.davidsonmorris.com/different-types-of-pay-structures/

EduFixers. (n.d). Human Resource Learning and Development Theories. https://edufixers.com/human-resource-learning-and-development-theories/

Elisabeth Kübler-Ross Foundation. (n.d). Kübler-Ross Change Curve. https://www.ekrfoundation.org/5-stages-of-grief/change-curve/

Executive Order, 11246 — Equal Employment Opportunity. Sept. 24, 1965, 30 FR 12319, 12935, 3 CFR, 1964–1965 Comp., P339. https://www.dol.gov/agencies/ofccp/executive-order-11246/as-amended#:~:text=Executive%20Order%2011246%20%E2%80%94%20Equal%20Employment%20Opportunity&text=24%2C%201965%2C%20appear%20at%2030,339%2C%20unless%20otherwise%20noted.

Express Analytics. (2021, September 10). The Complete Guide To Understanding Data Reporting. https://www.expressanalytics.com/blog/data-reporting/

First Up Blog. (n.d). What is employee communication and why it's more important than ever? https://firstup.io/blog/what-is-employee-communication-and-why-its-more-important-than-ever/

Forbes Coaches Council. (2020, June 8). 14 Top Tips For Dealing With Business Uncertainty. https://www.forbes.com/sites/forbescoachescouncil/2020/06/08/14-top-tips-for-dealing-with-business-uncertainty/?sh=2bce8c283b18

Gardner, Rhonda. (2022). Total Rewards Strategy. https://www.aihr.com/blog/total-rewards-strategy/?nowprocket=1

Garland, Stacie. (2022, August 7). Skill Testing. https://vervoe.com/skill-testing/

General Assembly, Illinois. (775 ILCS 5/). Illinois Human Rights Act. Illinois Gov., 02 Aug. 2021, https://dhr.illinois.gov/.

Guerin, Lisa. (2022). Types of Employment Contracts. https://www.nolo.com/legal-encyclopedia/types-employment-contracts.html

Henderson, Robert. (2022, September 9). What Is An ATS? 8 Things You Need to Know About Applicant Tracking Systems. https://www.jobscan.co/blog/8-things-you-need-to-know-about-applicant-tracking-systems/?iebrowser=1

Holliday, Marc. (2021, March 9). What Is Employee Retention? Benefits, Tips & Metrics. https://www.netsuite.com/portal/resource/articles/human-resources/employee-retention.shtml

HRCI. (2022). Certifications in Human Resources. https://www.hrci.org/docs/default-source/web-files/phr-exam-content-outline.pdf?sfvrsn=13c44f61_24

HR Help Board. (n.d). Employee Benefits Program of Organizations. https://www.hrhelpboard.com/hr-manual/employee-benefit-programs.htm

Human Resources MBA. (n.d). How Should Human Resources Participate in the Termination Process?

https://www.humanresourcesmba.net/faq/
how-should-human-resources-participate-in-the-termination-process/

iEduNote. (2022). 6 Elements of Organizational Structure.
https://www.iedunote.com/organizational-structure-elements

Ingram, David. (n.d) Payroll Accounting Procedures.
https://smallbusiness.chron.com/payroll-accounting-
procedures-4909.html

Jedox blog. (n.d). Reporting and Analysis.
https://www.jedox.com/en/blog/reporting-analysis/

Joubert, Shayna. (2020, September 30). Laws and Regulations Every HR
Professional Should Know.
https://www.northeastern.edu/graduate/blog/hr-laws-to-know/

Kempton, Beth. (2022). Guide to Alternative Solutions for Your
Staffing Needs.
https://www.upwork.com/resources/guide-alternative-staffing-solutions

Kenton, Will. (2022, November 28). Succession Planning Basics: How It
Works, Why It's Important.
https://www.investopedia.com/terms/s/succession-planning.asp

Kotter, J. P. *Leading Change*. Boston: Harvard Business School Press, 1996.

Kübler-Ross, Elisabeth. *On Death and Dying*. Macmillian Press, 1969.

Lalwani, Puja. (2020, August 10). What Is Performance Management?
Definition, Process, Cycle, and Best Practices for Planning.
https://www.spiceworks.com/hr/performance-management/articles/
what-is-performance-management/?nowprocket=1

Legal Information Institute. (n.d). Administrative Law.
https://www.law.cornell.edu/wex/administrative_law

Leonard, Kimberlee. (2018, October 25). Professional & Ethical Behavior in the Workplace. https://smallbusiness.chron.com/professional-ethical-behavior-workplace-10026.html

Management Study Guide. (n.d). Job analysis and job evaluation. https://www.managementstudyguide.com/job-analysis-and-job-evaluation.htm

Mayberry, Kate. (2016, October 24). The problem with being a long-term expat. https://www.bbc.com/worklife/article/20161024-the-problem-with-being-a-long-term-expat

Mckinsey. (2008, March 1). Enduring Ideas: The 7-S Framework https://www.mckinsey.com/capabilities/strategy-and-corporate-finance/our-insights/enduring-ideas-the-7-s-framework

McQuerrey, Lisa. (n.d). How to Evaluate an Employee's Attitude? https://smallbusiness.chron.com/evaluate-employees-attitude-10156.html

Michigan University Online. (2019, May 28). Understanding the Difference Between Quantitative and Qualitative Analytics. https://www.michiganstateuniversityonline.com/resources/business-analytics/difference-between-quantitative-and-qualitative-analytics/

Mind Tools for Business. (2015, June 11). Principles of Instructional Design. https://mindtoolsbusiness.com/resources/blog/principles-instructional-design

Mometrix Test Preparation. (2022, July 8). Adult Learning Processes and theories. https://www.mometrix.com/academy/adult-learning-processes-and-theories/

My Workplace Health. (2021, April 14). Understanding and Developing Organizational Culture.

https://myworkplacehealth.com/
understanding-and-developing-organizational-culture/

National Conference of State Legislatures. (2022). How States Define
Lobbying and Lobbyists.
https://www.ncsl.org/research/ethics/50-state-chart-lobby-
definitions.aspx

Occupational Safety and Health Administration. (1970). Occupational safety
and health standards: Occupational health and environmental control
(Standard No. 1910.95).
https://www.osha.gov/pls/
oshaweb/?p_table=STANDARDS&p_id=9735.

Ohio State University. (n.d). Accident Prevention in the Workplace.
https://ehs.osu.edu/accident-prevention-workplace

Open Libraries. (n.d). Collective Bargaining.
https://open.lib.umn.edu/humanresourcemanagement/
chapter/12-2-collective-bargaining/

Open Libraries. (n.d). Designing a training program.
https://open.lib.umn.edu/humanresourcemanagement/
chapter/8-4-designing-a-training-program/

Open Libraries. (n.d). The law and recruitment.
https://open.lib.umn.edu/humanresourcemanagement/
chapter/4-2-the-law-and-recruitment/

Open Libraries. (n.d). The Roles of Mission, Vision, and Values.
https://open.lib.umn.edu/principlesmanagement/
chapter/4-3-the-roles-of-mission-vision-and-values/

Passemall. (2022, May 16). PHR Pass Rate: What Is The Passing Score For
PHR in 2023?
https://passemall.com/phr-pass-rate-what-is-the-passing-score-for-phr/

Passemall. (2022, May 16). What Are PHR Certification Requirements? [2023 Updated]
https://passemall.com/what-are-phr-certification-requirement-updated/

Pearson Education. (2022). Introduction to Compensation and Benefit Design: Applying Finance and Accounting Principles to Global Human Resource Management Systems.
https://www.informit.com/articles/article.aspx?p=2002833&seqNum=4

Petryni, Matt. (2019, February 1). The Importance of Human Relations in the Workplace.
https://smallbusiness.chron.com/importance-human-relations-workplace-23061.html

Privacy Research Team. (2022, August 26). The HR Guide to Employee Data Protection.
https://securiti.ai/blog/hr-employee-data-protection/

Reid, Stephanie. (n.d). Labour Relations Law.
https://smallbusiness.chron.com/labor-relations-law-56417.html

Reynolds, Sarah. (2019, April 9). Non-Monetary Compensation, Explained.
https://www.salary.com/blog/non-monetary-compensation-explained/

Sands, Bill. (2020, October). Tips & Tricks for Your Upcoming PHR Certification Exam.
https://study.com/blog/tips-tricks-for-your-upcoming-phr-certification-exam.html

SIB Blog. (2022). HR role in disaster recovery planning.
https://www.stayinbusiness.com/hr-role-in-disaster-recovery-planning/

SHRM (2022) Screening and Evaluating Job Candidates.
https://www.shrm.org/resourcesandtools/tools-and-samples/toolkits/pages/screeningandevaluatingcandidates.aspx

Smart Recruiters. (n.d). Talent Pool.
https://www.smartrecruiters.com/resources/glossary/talent-pool/

Smith, Mark. (2022, July 21). How Exam Preparation Benefits You—and Your
Organization.
https://www.shrm.org/resourcesandtools/hr-topics/behavioral-
competencies/pages/how-exam-preparation-benefits-you-and-your-
organization.aspx

Stevenson, Cliff. (2013, April 10). The 10 best ways HR can improve workplace
creativity and innovation.
https://www.i4cp.com/trendwatchers/2013/04/10/
the-10-best-ways-hr-can-improve-workplace-creativity-and-innovation

Study Guide Zone. (2022, October 17). PHR Exam.
https://www.studyguidezone.com/phr.htm

Thaler, R. H & Sunstein, C. R. *Nudge: Improving Decisions About Health, Wealth
and Happiness*. Penguin Publisher, 2008.

TPI Group Inc. (2019). What Is Corporate Governance and Compliance?
https://www.tpigroupinc.com/
what-is-corporate-governance-compliance/

United States House of Representatives. (n.d). The Legislative Process.
https://www.house.gov/the-house-explained/the-legislative-process

United States Congress. 99th Congress, 2nd Session, 1986. Public Law 99-272.
Consolidated Omnibus Budget Reconciliation Act of 1985.
https://www.govinfo.gov/app/details/STATUTE-100/
STATUTE-100-Pg82/summary

United States Congress. 2427. The Employee Retirement Income Security Act
of 1974 (ERISA). 29 U.S.C. 1001 Et Seq.
https://www.dol.gov/agencies/ebsa/laws-and-regulations/laws/erisa

United States Congress. The Fair Labor Standards Act of 1938 As Amended.

Rev. May 2011 Rev. May 2011 ed. U.S. Dept. of Labor Wage and Hour Division 2011.
http://purl.fdlp.gov/GPO/gpo24709

United States Congress. The Family and Medical Leave Act of 1993, 29 U.S.C. §§ 2601–2654 (2006).
https://www.govinfo.gov/app/details/FR-1995-01-06/94-32342/summary

United States Congress. United States Code: Immigration and Nationality, 8 U.S.C. §§ -1401 Suppl. 2 1964. 1964. Periodical. Retrieved from the Library of Congress. <www.loc.gov/item/uscode1964-016008006/>.

United States Congress. Health Insurance Portability and Accountability Act [HIPAA] of 1996, Pub. L. No. 104-191.
https://www.govinfo.gov/content/pkg/PLAW-104publ191/pdf/PLAW-104publ191.pdf

United States Congress, House. S.1200 - 99th Congress (1985-1986): Immigration Reform and Control Act of 1986." Congress.gov, Library of Congress, 6 November 1986. https://www.congress.gov/bill/99th-congress/senate-bill/1200.

United States Congress. Patient Protection and Affordable Care Act of 2010, Pub. L. No. 111–148, 124 Stat. 119 (2010), Codified as Amended 42 U.S.C. § 18001.
https://www.govinfo.gov/app/details/STATUTE-124/STATUTE-124-Pg119/context

United States Congress. Public Law 107–56—OCT. 26, 2001. Uniting and Strengthening America by Providing Appropriate Tools Required to Intercept and Obstruct Terrorism (USA PATRIOT ACT) Act of 2001.
https://www.congress.gov/107/plaws/publ56/PLAW-107publ56.pdf

United States Congress. Public Law. 88-38, 1963. Equal Pay Act of 1963 (EPA).
https://www.eeoc.gov/statutes/equal-pay-act-1963

United States Congress. Public Law 90-202, 1967. The Age Age Discrimination in Employment Act of 1967 (ADEA). https://www.eeoc.gov/statutes/ age-discrimination-employment-act-1967

United States Congress. S.933 — 101st Congress (1989-1990). Americans with Disabilities Act of 1990 (ADA). https://www.congress.gov/bill/101st-congress/senate-bill/933

United States Congress. Public Law 95-555, 1978. Pregnancy Discrimination Act (PDA). https://www.dol.gov/agencies/oasam/civil-rights-center/internal/ policies/pregnancy-discrimination#:~:text=The%20Pregnancy%20 Discrimination%20Act%20of,childbirth%2C%20or%20related%20 medical%20conditions.

United States Congress. (Pub. L. 88-352) Title VII of the Civil Rights Act. U.S. Equal Employment Opportunity Commission, 15 Oct. 1964. https://www.eeoc.gov/statutes/title-vii-civil-rights-act-1964.

University of Illinois Board of Trustees. (2022). Major laws and regulations for the selection process. https://www.hr.uillinois.edu/policy/compliance_toolkit/ major_laws_and_regulations_for_selection_process

University of Michigan Medical School. (2022). Ways to Transition Staff Smoothly During Periods of Change. https://faculty.medicine.umich.edu/ ways-transition-staff-smoothly-during-periods-change

U.S. Congress. United States Code: National Labor Relations, 29 U.S.C. §§ 151-166 Suppl. 2. 1934. Periodical. Retrieved from the Library of Congress, <www.loc.gov/item/uscode1934-003029007/>.

U.S. Equal Employemnt Opportunity Commission. (n.d). Laws Enforced by EEOC. https://www.eeoc.gov/statutes/laws-enforced-eeoc

Verlinden, Neelie. (2022). All You Need To Know About Employee Relations.
https://www.aihr.com/blog/employee-relations/?nowprocket=1

Verlinden, Neelie. (2022). Employee Orientation.
https://www.aihr.com/blog/new-employee-orientation/?nowprocket=1

Verma, Eshna. (2022, November 22). How to Measure Training Effectiveness in 2023.
https://www.simplilearn.com/
how-to-measure-effectiveness-corporate-training-article

Vulpen, Erik. (2022). How To Conduct a Training Needs Analysis.
https://www.aihr.com/blog/training-needs-analysis/?nowprocket=1

Vulpen, Erik. (2022). Recruiting Metrics.
https://www.aihr.com/blog/recruiting-metrics/?nowprocket=1

Wadsworth, William. (2021, March 31). 41 Powerful Study Motivation Quotes For Exam Success.
https://examstudyexpert.com/study-motivation-quotes/

Western Governor's University. (2020, March 20). What is Risk Management in Business?
https://www.wgu.edu/blog/what-risk-management-business2003.
html#close

Workforce Hub. (2022, April 19). Create a Study Plan to Pass the PHR Certification Test [and SHRM-CP].
https://www.workforcehub.com/blog/everything-you-need-to-know-to-pass-the-phr-certification-test/?nowprocket=1

Your Article Library. (n.d). Top 9 Techniques of Organisation Development.
https://www.yourarticlelibrary.com/hrm/organisation/
top-9-techniques-of-organisation-development/60275